To my friend Nowsey
Best of Luck

David Cohen

The Trailer Twins

THE HARREL & DARREL COHRON STORY

The Cohron Family

Hudson Books

Book design by:
Arbor Books, Inc.
www.arborbooks.com

Printed in Canada

The Trailer Twins: The Harrel and Darrel Cohron Story
The Cohron Family

1. Title   2. Author   3. Memoir

Library of Congress Control Number: 2010927212

ISBN 13: 978-0-9822553-4-6

Table of Contents

We would like to dedicate this book to the loves of our lives, the ones who kept us straight and kept the home fires burning, **Joan Cohron and Shirley Cohron.**

Acknowledgments

We would like to offer a huge "thank you" to Mike Michaels for turning us on to mobile homes way back when.

We also need to say a heartfelt "thank you" to our many employees; we couldn't have done it without all of you: Leroy Reynolds, Al Williams, John Burdine, Dick Braun, Leonard Cohron, Missey DeLore, Don Poteat, Scott Cooper, Rick Moore, Carol Turner, Carina Moreno, Lee Compton, Dick Evans, Don Twomey, Jim Scott, Leroy Sexton, Liz Riester, Orlando Raney, Bill Stout, Ed Carroll, Pearl Brown, Nancy Koch, Bob Woodhouse, Garnett Hite, Terry Twomey, Walt Beecher, Mary Helmling, Dave Potter, Gary Guzenda, Bobby Cooper, Pam Robinson, Eric Eastin, Harry Pitts, Lonnie Immel, Larry Creek, Harold Weller, Bill Sexton, Helen Smith, John Roberts, Mike Turner, Scott McCurdy, Matt Cooper, Gwen Troxell, Stu Goar and Matt Parker.

We are sorry to any whom we might have left off of this list.

Also, we need to thank our many subcontractors, CPAs,

legal advisors and manufacturers and their reps that we have worked with over the years.

Thanks for all the great memories.

—Harrel and Darrel

Foreword

My name is Matt Cohron, and I have the pleasure of introducing you to my grandfather, Darrel Cohron, and his twin brother, Harrel. They are amazing men, and anyone who knows them will be able to tell you a story (or two or three or four) about their kindness, their generosity and their love of pranks. Darrel and Harrel both are colorful characters who are a lot of fun to be around. They also taught me a lot about the world of business and the real world, about how to treat people and how to take care of a family.

These two brothers had interesting childhoods, to say the least, and family always was a high priority to them. They also are incredible businessmen who built a lasting empire from scratch. What sets them apart from so many others is that they were able to combine what they loved—their family and their business—into a livelihood that still prospers today.

My dad, his siblings and their cousins all grew up with the family business. I did, too, as did my siblings and cousins. We might all have been born with the Cohron work ethic, or maybe it was instilled in us through osmosis; I'm not really sure. I simply know that we all love being a part of what Darrel and Harrel created.

These days, Grandpa and Harrel have pretty much retired from the day-to-day operations of the business, but they're still around. They love it too much to stay away. My dad and his cousins run the show now, and I have joined in. I'm the first of the third generation to join the family business.

If you live around Indianapolis, Indiana, you might know the name Cohron. Grandpa and Harrel launched their business way back in 1955 and it still thrives today, right on the same road. If you are not familiar with Indy, though, it doesn't matter. At its heart, this book is about identical twin brothers who came from nothing and symbolize the American success story. It's an interesting tale no matter what.

We could call this a business book, as Darrel and Harrel lived the epitome of a "rags to riches" story, and they are savvy entrepreneurs. We could call it a memoir because this is their life story. We could call this book a lot of things, but mainly, to us, it is a family album, a means of documenting Harrel and Darrel Cohron's lives, loves and genius. For those in the family who are still too young to know and appreciate these two brilliant gentlemen, we wanted to capture their tales and keep the memories alive. Past, present and future generations of our family need to know these stories—as do people outside of the family. Everyone, we believe, will enjoy getting to know the brothers, their crazy, good-natured antics and their secrets to million-dollar success.

The coming pages contain the stories that Darrel and Harrel allowed us to share, though I have a hunch that there were a few doozies they chose to leave out. The information was collected from many, many folks who know these two wild and crazy guys, and I would like to extend a big thank you to all who took part in this project. Whether your contribution was large or small, it is much appreciated.

Because this book is such a huge collaborative effort, no one person can claim author credit. We hired a writer to help us put it all together, my dad, Bobby Cohron, and my uncle, Brad Cohron, were the driving forces behind getting the book done. We all tossed around titles—it could simply have been called *Our Life* by Harrel Cohron and Darrel Cohron, but they didn't want their names on it or a lot of hoopla—and drew straws to see whose name got to grace this foreword page. Obviously, I won.

However, there are many others we have to acknowledge. Of course, there's Bill, Karen and Sheila Cohron, and my sister and all our cousins. There's also all the staff and our many wonderful friends who are really like family, including Woody, Liz and Leroy. And, certainly, there would be no generations of Cohrons if not for my grandmother, Shirley, and Harrel's wife, Joan—two best friends who married twins.

Harrel and Darrel Cohron might have looked alike and had similar-sounding names, but their personalities diverged enough to run a business together. They also recognized each other's strengths and allowed each other the space to run differing sides of the business.

That is not to say that they always agreed. Actually, their spats are legendary. However, the feuds never lasted long and the brothers maintained a successful business for more than four decades. For the Indy locals, if you drive down Pendleton

Pike and see the big ol' cow statue, that's where you'll find Cohron's Manufactured Homes. Stop in! And if you've never been to Indiana, make a trip. In June, we have a strawberry festival for all our homeowners. In December, we have a huge barn party for the whole community. Those traditions are parts of who we are.

Harrel and Darrel agreed to do this project not because they wanted a book about themselves—they didn't. We had to convince them that it was not really for them but for their grandkids. Ah, the grandkids. That changed everything.

We also wanted to get the truth out there about mobile-home parks. Many people have preconceived notions about manufactured homes and we would like to put all those negative myths to rest. For those of you who hear the term and automatically think "trailer trash," think again. Obviously, you have never been to a Cohron Mobile Home Park.

Harrel and Darrel took great pride in the cleanliness and condition of each mobile home and the entire grounds of each park they owned. Community pride was very important to them—just as important as personal pride. Both were evident in all of our parks and everything we do.

My grandpa, Darrel, and his brother, Harrel, showed that a person can be full of pride and still be humble. They are two gracious gentlemen who treat everyone with dignity and respect and never lost their Southern charm. Harrel and Darrel always set a good example—one that I follow every single day of my life.

It is my privilege and honor to share these stories with you. Savor the moments, as they are too soon gone.

Please enjoy, and do stop in to say hello.

— Matt Cohron, on behalf of the entire Cohron family
Cohron's Manufactured Home Communities
9622 Pendleton Pike
Indianapolis, Indiana

A Note From the Mayor

Harrel and Darrel Cohron are the true great leaders of the City of Lawrence. They have served as a rock-solid foundation through the years, as Lawrence has grown from a sleepy, little suburb of Indianapolis to the fifteenth-largest city in the state of Indiana. The success of Lawrence is directly attributable to the support, faith, and leadership that Harrel and Darrel have shown to this community and its citizens.

In 1954, the Cohrons started a business that grew to become one of the largest—if not the largest—in the entire state. They toiled endlessly to provide for their families and to serve a large portion of our citizens with their business, which was built on foresight, hard work and their belief in their fellow man. Though there was much criticism of and disdain for trailers, the Cohron brothers provided mobile *homes* for many, many people from all walks of life. The several mobile-home parks in which they invested were the epitomes of class and cleanliness and enjoyed great reputations throughout the industry.

Yes, Harrel and Darrel worked hard, but man, did they play hard as well! The practical jokes they played on each other and their friends are legendary. One time, a Lawrence police officer told Harrel to leave a field where he was hunting for rabbits, as it was not approved hunting land. Of course, Harrel took off, but he went and told Darrel that the hunting was great in this field. So, Darrel grabbed his gun and went right over. Imagine his surprise when the officer threatened to arrest him, since he had already been told to leave. Oh, the joys of being a twin.

I have another fond memory of Harrel and Darrel wrasslin' in the gravel of their sales lot, both dressed in suits. They called such altercations their "board meetings." When they were through, they brushed themselves off, and we all went to dinner. As much as their "friendly" discussions were legendary, no two siblings ever had greater love for one another than they did.

The number of charities, good causes, friends, strangers, the city, people in general that benefitted from the monetary and moral support of the Cohron brothers is countless. Harrel and Darrel were and are true believers in humanity, and they've brought success to any number of charitable causes simply by participating in them.

Husbands, fathers, corporate leaders and good ol' boys, Harrel and Darrel have always lived their lives and met their responsibilities to the best of their abilities. For that reason, they are top among the true success stories in the City of Lawrence. With love and respect, I am glad to be a part of the wonderfully rich and full fabric of the lives of Harrel and Darrel Cohron.

Respectfully,
Mayor Paul Ricketts
Lawrence, Indiana

Chapter 1

"Trailers for sale or rent…" The classic tune "King of the Road" might be the theme song of legendary country singer Roger Miller, but it's also near and dear to the hearts of the Cohron family. Brothers Harrel and Darrel Cohron would never in a million years call themselves royalty, but they are the undisputed kings of *their* road, Pendleton Pike/ Route 67 in Lawrence, Indiana, a suburb of Indianapolis.

Their reign of popularity comes not just from having been in business in the same spot for over fifty years, or from the huge statue of a cow in the front parking lot, or even from their being such good businessmen. All of that is true, no question there, but the secret to their success is simple: They treat people the way they would want to be treated themselves.

"It's just plain old common sense," they would say, because that's how Harrel and Darrel Cohron view the world. It's also the way they run their business and their lives.

Still, there's nothing common about these two brothers. On the outside, they might seem like ordinary, everyday folks but in reality, they—and their business—are exceptional.

The Cohrons sold their first used trailer back in 1955, and that led to another and then another, and so on and so on.

These days, Cohron's Manufactured Home Communities is a multimillion-dollar business that includes six Florida-style mobile-home communities and offers financing, insurance and service to the homes they sell. The company has become an Indiana landmark and a legacy that extends beyond just the Cohron family. Harrel and Darrel have certainly passed on their knowledge and beliefs to their children and grand-children, but they have also touched the lives of everybody they've met.

As identical twins, Harrel and Darrel Cohron have always been partners. Born on November 11, 1932, they grew up in Morgantown, Kentucky, a typical, rural Southern community with a small-town feel. Morgantown was populated by hard-working folks, maybe 400 or so, who tended their farms and knew all their neighbors up and down the town's gravel roads. It's no wonder the boys later developed such a strong interest in community building.

These days, The Cohron brothers call Pendleton Pike in Lawrence, Indiana, their home—or, at least, the home of their business. The highway is certainly no gravel road, but Harrel and Darrel know just about everybody in the area anyway, as well as pretty much everyone else in the community. Lawrence, with its 40,000 residents, is much larger than Morgantown had been, but the Cohron brothers treat it just the same. People are people, they figure, no matter how many of them there are.

The number of people in Lawrence and greater Indianapolis could be partially attributed to the Cohrons themselves, who have done their share of populating the area through their trailer business—and through the building of their own families. Harrel married his wife, Joan, in 1955 and they had three children, Bill, Brad and Karen; Darrel married his wife, Shirley, in 1956 and they had two children, Sheila and Bobby. These days, Harrel has seven grandchildren and three great grandchildren, and Darrel has five and three, respectively. The entire Cohron clan lives in the Indianapolis area and each member has spent his or her share of hours on the Cohron Homes' lot or in its office. The business has always been a backdrop in their lives.

"My dad worked long hours. That's just the way it was back then," explains Bobby Cohron, Darrel's son. "We didn't think anything about it. The sales lot was open seven days a week—that was normal. My dad took off half a day on Thursdays and only worked from noon until six on Sundays. That was his only time off."

Brad Cohron, Harrel's second son, concurs. "My dad and Darrel worked a lot, there's no doubt about that, but my dad always had time for us. We went camping a lot. I remember lots of fun times on the weekends. We spent plenty of time together as a family."

"My dad would get home at nine at night, but he was never too tired to spend time with us," Bobby remembers. "He never complained about work. My dad was happy to go—but he was also happy to come home. Every night, we would load up in the car, me and my sister in our pajamas, and go for a ride to the old-fashioned root beer stand in town, where car hops would bring trays out to the car. We loved to go there. We would get root beer floats or Cokes, and then my folks would take us for a drive through their parks. That was our routine just about every night."

Bobby—as well as all the other Cohron children—remembers a childhood with his dad and uncle that was full of hunting and fishing, camping, boating and, of course, the business, all intermingled. Above all else, the Cohrons knew that Darrel and Harrel loved what they did for a living, and none of them could imagine it being any other way.

Patriarch Darrel confirms this: "We loved it. We still do. You have to. If you're not in love with what you do, you're just not ever gonna make it."

Chapter 2

From the first moments of their lives, Harrel and Darrel have enjoyed a pretty traditional sibling rivalry—though their version of it has an interesting twist. While most twins are born only a matter of minutes apart, second-born Darrel kept his brother waiting quite a bit longer for his debut.

"My mother was a big woman," Harrel explains, "and back then they didn't have the ultrasound machines that they do now. So the doctor didn't know that there was another baby in there! Our mother did not know that she was carrying twins. So, I was born, and then an hour and a half later, Darrel came out—*an hour and a half later.*"

Harrel and Darrel were the last in a long line of children born to Ben and Clyde Cohron, including brothers Getty, Paul, Leonard and Glen (who was, tragically, stillborn) and two sisters, Louise and Sarah Dean—or just plain "Dean," as she was called. Dean was and still is incredibly close to Harrel and Darrel; as the oldest girl in the family, she was responsible for a lot of the childcare duties and in truth was somewhat of a second mother to the boys. Now eighty-nine years old, Dean lives in Lawrence along with the rest of the clan, and is still in possession of all the vim and vigor inherent in the Cohron blood. She even still takes a walk every day, even if it's just laps in her home, going from room to room.

Dean always lights up when talking about the twins and the joy she experienced from helping raise them in the past. Bringing out a current photo of them, she proudly shows it off, her smile wide. "Look," she says, pointing to the picture. "They still dress alike."

And this is true. In photo after photo, Harrel and Darrel are shown in similar clothing, with similar hairstyles to match their identical faces. Their tastes are eerily—but understandably—alike, even when they don't intend them to be. At a recent family Christmas party, they both showed up separately in nearly identical red sweaters. For their fiftieth birthday party, they went shopping alone but came home with the exact same suits. Throughout their lives this has happened to them time and time again—they buy suits or shoes or shirts that are exactly alike except for the color or some other small detail. The twin connection is real with these two, and simply a part of who they are.

In gratitude for all the many years that Dean acted as a mother figure in their lives, Darrel and Harrel now take care of her, and have never stopped showing her their appreciation. Nine years ago, for her eightieth birthday, they even gave her a double-wide trailer to live in. Sitting in its kitchen, reminiscing over the old photographs, she can't help but grin. "They're still my babies," she reports.

Dean remembers quite vividly when the twins were born. She was eleven, and she says that the first days following the birth were tense.

"Darrel couldn't digest his milk, and back then, it was common for one twin to die. We called a granny woman to the house to help and she told us to milk a cow, just one udder, and feed that milk to Darrel."

So, they borrowed a cow. "We milked twice a day," Dean recalls. "It was only boiled cow's milk for those babies. Mother did not breastfeed. All we had for them was two bottles apiece. We didn't have a refrigerator. We would put the milk in pails and keep them in the flowing spring in the cave that was on our farm, just under the hill. The spring water kept the milk cool enough to keep it fresh. I can still picture the cave and the spring. I know that we used to do our laundry in that spring, too, so we didn't have to carry water back up the hill to the house. It was easier to take the laundry down there. "

As for the initial scare with the babies, the granny woman and the cow's milk did the trick. After about six weeks, Darrel was gaining weight and thriving—and even eating solid food. "I gave them both hard biscuits with warm water, sugar, and Karo syrup," Dean says, remarking that it might be why they both have such sweet tooths today.

"We only had twelve diapers when Harrel and Darrel were born," Dean continues, remembering all the details like it all happened yesterday. "I had to boil the diapers with lye. Laundry was put out to dry on the clothes line and tossed over on the bushes. No one had clothes dryers back then. We made our own diapers then, too. With a bolt of fabric, I could make forty-eight diapers. I cut the squares and hemmed them on our mother's sewing machine. You had to fold them catty wampus like so—" She demonstrates. "And pin them like this. We also pinned their leg stockings to the diapers. The stockings would get wet, too, of course. I'd just throw them on the fire rack to dry. The stockings, not the twins."

In those days, taking care of babies, and especially twins, was hard work. But, Dean didn't see it that way. Back then, she asserted, people did what they had to do and didn't think twice about it. She enjoyed her time with the boys when they were young and still enjoys spending time with them to this day. At seventy-six, Darrel and Harrel are still the apples of Dean's eye—although she remembers lots of mischief, such as the time when they threw wet corn cobs at her when they were little boys. They were pistols from the beginning; personality and perseverance were their birthrights.

However, not everything was fun and games during their childhoods. It was the Depression era, and money was in short supply. Times were tough for everyone; all the families in Morgantown, where they were raised, were in the same economic boat. Perhaps it was this sense of community that got the Cohron family through the rough times.

"Those were the days when Kentucky only had horse-drawn fire trucks," Dean recalls. "And kerosene lamps. We might not have had electricity, but we sure had fun. We were poor as could be, but we were comfortable."

During the Depression, many families found themselves not just low on money but short on food as well. With so many children to care for, this could have been a real dilemma in the Cohron household. But, according to Dean, they managed.

"We always had enough to eat," she reports. "I won't say

that we always had enough to wear, but we got by. We wore each other's stuff. I wore more boy clothes than girl clothes because there were more boys in the family and we had more boy clothes!"

However, after losing both their parents when Harrel and Darrel were quite young, the Cohron family found themselves scraping to get by. "We lived on a farm," Dean explains. "When Daddy was alive, he had a sharecropper, and Daddy worked for Butler County as a road grader. We were never wealthy, but without him, during the Depression, it was even worse. Money was not a part of the twins' childhoods."

Still, Dean insists, their childhoods were happy. "We were as happy as June bugs," she says. "We played Annie over and hide and seek. We grew peanuts and popcorn and pears and apples. We shelled beans for the winter. When we were bad, our punishment was to separate the dark beans out from the white beans. In the summertime, the boys went fishing and played ball."

Dean loves to be the family storyteller—and doesn't mind spilling a few family secrets. "Our mom was as good as gold," she reports.

In contrast, Dean had a very special relationship with her father: "I thought my daddy hung the moon and set the sun. I was real close with my daddy. He was made out of gold. Too bad the twins never got to know him. He died on the twenty-second of July. Mama died the twenty-second of January. As a matter of fact, many years later, my husband, Walter, had to go into the service on the twenty-second of July as well. Another year, a tornado ripped through the farm on the twenty-second of June, and our barn burnt down on another twenty-second of July." Pausing, she laughs. "I used to pray every month for the Lord to get me through the twenty-second day."

After Dean got married, she moved to Indiana with her husband, leaving her siblings behind in Kentucky. However, although she was happy in her new surroundings, she couldn't get Darrel and Harrel off of her mind.

"I wanted to give those boys a chance," she says. "I wanted to give them an education. I couldn't sleep at night after I moved here. I wanted Harrel and Darrel to get out of Butler County and make something of themselves. Walter and I let them live here, and they went to high school—they were the only ones out of all of us who did. I would say they made something of themselves. Just look at them now."

Chapter 3

As twins, Harrel and Darrel have always had a love/hate relationship. But, their love for the business, their families, their employees and their customers has always been straightforward and without a doubt.

However, even to use the word "employees" to describe those who work at Cohron's Manufactured Home Communities is not quite right. Since Darrel and Harrel started the business, the people who have worked for them have become their friends and, ultimately, even like family. Because of their business and personal ethics and their great personalities, Darrel and Harrel have won a great deal of loyalty from those in their employ, and that loyalty goes both ways—as bosses, the Cohrons are very invested not just in their company but in its people. They understand that to make a business thrive, you have to keep the people who are doing the work as satisfied as possible.

Unfortunately, that's not how it goes in many workplaces today. Too many people in too many companies just punch the clock and gripe about their jobs and their bosses. But that never happens at Cohron's Homes. The staff there knows that they will be taken care of, and so they work hard to create solid relationships with their customers and maintain the quality atmosphere that is the Cohron trademark.

The longevity of the business and the extremely low rate of staff turnover are testaments to what it's like to work there, but that does not mean that the Cohron brothers are pushovers. They treat their people well, but they demand a lot of them. Just ask Woody—a.k.a. longtime employee Bob Woodhouse—who likes to tell a story about one time when he and Harrel were out eating lunch.

While chatting with a local farmer at the restaurant, Harrel patted Woody on the shoulder and told the farmer, "Woody here has worked for me for thirty-eight years, and I have never given him a paid vacation."

The farmer shrugged and replied, "Now, Harrel, I don't think I would be bragging about that."

Woody enjoys that story—and, more importantly, he genuinely enjoyed his nearly four decades at Cohron's Homes. These days, he's retired, but he still helps out occasionally if the brothers ever need him, and he loves to reminisce about the early days of working on the Cohron sales lot.

"It was a different era back then when I first started," he remembers. "We worked hard and we partied hard. You might say we were wild back in the day. Times in general have changed. Back then, we had company parties and everyone smoked and we played cards and we had bands playing. The parties would go until two or three in the morning. This past year's Christmas party was certainly more tame. No one smokes anymore, and there was no band. The whole party was over by nine-thirty, I think."

Back then, everyone at Cohron's Homes put in many long hours, but they loved what they did—and when you love what you do, the money follows. That's a concept that seems to have gotten lost in today's business world.

"Harrel and Darrel were and are great businessmen," Woody remembers. "There's no doubt about that. But the real secret to their success is that they are great people. I think they're a perfect example of rags to riches, and I bet I could write an entire book of stories about them all by myself. I've loved every minute of my time with them. It was a hell of a ride, that is for sure."

Woody had been the treasurer and manager of the Finance Center Federal Credit Union for about fifteen years when he met Harrel and Darrel At the time, Indianapolis' military base, Ft. Benjamin Harrison, had its own mobile-home park; the Cohrons sold the homes, and the credit union did the financing. If a serviceman who bought a Cohron home got transferred overseas and could not keep the home but was not able to sell it, the credit union would get it back. That was where Woody came in—he would let Harrel and Darrel know about such situations and if they had a customer who was interested, they would send him over to refinance the repossessed home instead of selling him a more-expensive new one.

"If my memory serves me right," Woody notes, "the credit union never lost any money on the homes we financed that way. Darrel and Harrel were sincere and honest when it came to taking care of the companies that did the financing of the mobile homes they sold. They are good men."

And, it seems, good friends. Through doing business with Cohrons, Woody became drinking buddies with Harrel and as often happens, the social relationship eventually turned to business.

"One night when we were out having a good time," Woody recalls, "he told me that his salesman had left and that they were looking to replace him. Now, I really enjoyed my job. I'd just finished a five-year project—opening the first branch of Finance Center Federal Credit Union overseas, in Germany. But when Harrel said there was an opening at his company, I was interested. So, I asked him about it. And he asked me why I would want to leave such a good job to come sell mobile homes. I told him that I just wanted to do something different."

True to his nature, even though he knew that Woody would have been a great asset at Cohron Homes, Harrel tried to talk Woody out of it. But, Woody persisted, and eventually he did go to work for the Cohrons.

"Little did I know what I was getting into," Woody recalls with a laugh. "Harrel sat me at my desk that first day and said, 'I'm going to give you a pen, a sales book, a payment book, credit applications and twenty-five percent of all the profit you make on every sale you make. But don't ask for anything else."

He didn't, and that was how he ended up with no paid vacation.

But the Cohrons made it up to him in other ways. Lee

Compton, the sales manager, told him that if I didn't make at least $20,000 a year, Lee would make up the difference himself, and in 1968 that was good money. Fortunately, by April of his first year at Cohron Homes, Woody had made as much money as he had at the credit union in a year.

Still, his time there wasn't always so perfect. "After I'd been working there about three months," he recalls, "I went out and bought a used home for us to fix up and sell. As the Cohron's truck hauled it into our sales lot, I could see that the home was all rusted and leaned to one side. *Oh, man,* I thought, *what have I done?* I had bought the thing at night and hadn't seen any of its imperfections. I'd thought I was doing a good thing."

Unfortunately, Darrel was standing in the lot office as the truck went by, and he saw the home in all its rundown glory. He looked at Harrel and then at Woody and asked, "Who hired that dumb SOB?"

And that wasn't the end of his misery. During that first year, at the end of each month, Woody had to figure out the profit on the deals he'd sold and turn them in to get his paycheck. One month, when figuring one of his deals, he realized that he had sold it for cost and made no profit on it at all. He had sold it for the invoice price, which was what the Cohrons had paid for the home. And it had been a cash deal, so he didn't even make any money on the financing.

Terrified of what Harrel would say, Woody went into his office expecting the worst.

"I made a mistake, boss," he said, and explained what he had done.

After hearing him out, Harrel sat back in his chair, behind his desk, and contemplated for a moment. "Did you learn anything from this?" he finally asked.

Bowing his head in embarrassment, Woody replied, "I learned to slow down and double check my figures before I give a customer a price."

Nodding, Harrel had smiled. "Then this isn't a mistake. It's a lesson learned. Next time…it *will* be a mistake."

Rest assured, there never was a next time for Woody.

As he came to learn, making mistakes was usually okay with Harrel and Darrel, as long as he was honest about what had happened. They also expected him to be honest with their customers, and not to take advantage of any situation. One of the many things that Woody admired about both the brothers was that they expected their employees to make profits, but if anyone tried to squeeze *too* much profit out of a customer, they would get in as much trouble as if they hadn't made a profit at all. In stark contrast to today's business world, even back then the Cohrons proved you could have ethics and still have enormous bottom-line success.

Part of this success came from the trust that they put in their employees. They always let their salesmen figure their own deals; they were there if anyone needed help, but otherwise they left it up to the staff to handle all the sales.

"I really appreciated that," Woody says, "and I think the customers did, too. I've always hated when a salesman has to get a manager to give you a deal. What do you need salespeople for if they can't make deals on their own? Without that power, they're just *show*men, as in, 'Let me show you what we have'—not *sales*men. I'll never understand that kind of thinking and that's why I loved selling at Cohrons, because I was truly a salesman. It felt good knowing that Harrel and Darrel had enough confidence in their salesmen to let them actually sell instead of just show the homes."

For fifteen years Woody and the Cohron brothers worked from 7:30 a.m. to 9:00 p.m. seven days a week—except on Tuesdays and Sundays, when Woody was allowed to go in at noon. Back in the day, business was booming; at one point, they sold over 600 homes in one year. Woody averaged twenty-five to thirty homes a month by himself, and the company delivered four homes a day. On Saturdays and Sundays, they would have fifty to seventy-five customer cars at a time on the sales lot.

It would get so busy, in fact, that the Cohrons and Woody had to devise a system so they would know who had been talked with and who needed follow up. To do this, they used red and green yardsticks: After talking to customers, if they were not potential sales at that time or could not qualify to buy a home, we would give them red yardsticks; if we thought that there might be a chance for a sale, we gave them green yardsticks. The customers did not know the significance of the colors; they were simply told that it was a way to let the staff know that someone had already talked to them.

"That was our explanation to them, and that was the truth," Woody says. "We had lots of people to talk to and wanted to be able to make contact with everyone who stopped in."

But there were times when they just went gangbusters, Woody reports. "It was nuts. We stocked over one hundred models at one time on the sales lot. Try to picture that: one hundred mobile homes all in one place. That's a lot of inventory. Those were crazy times."

As was the competition. At one time back, there were over thirty-eight mobile-home sales lots in Indianapolis.

"I learned one thing early in my sales career," Woody notes. "You always sell yourself first, then the product. Even if you happen to be a little higher priced than your competitor, the customer will still buy from you if they like you."

In time, however, things slowed down, and there were fewer customers coming into the sales lot. At that point, the Cohrons talked about closing on Sundays, but Woody fought this decision hard. "I thought that Sunday was one of our best sales days. I lost the fight, but it turned out to be a good choice. The Cohrons were smart business owners."

And that genius spread to all aspects of their organization. Harrel was a wiz with paperwork and financing, and with business practices in general.

"We didn't floor plan any of our homes," Woody remembers, "which means that the Cohrons paid cash outright for the mobile homes when they came from the factory. This made us more competitive because we didn't have floor-plan interest charges that we would have to pass on to the customers."

From the beginning, the Cohrons handled only the best-quality homes, which made for more-satisfied customers and less service problems. "That's a win-win," Woody says. "The price was sometimes a little bit higher than our competitors', but we were able to educate our customers about the value they received. People who bought from us understood that they were getting nicer homes."

While other dealers had hard times financing their homes, Harrel had always had a good relationship with the local banks and could get excellent financing arrangements through them. The Cohrons looked out for any lending institutions who worked with them, so any losses were held to a minimum.

"We did business with First Bank of Elkhart, Indiana National Bank, Merchant's National Bank and others," says Woody. "No other dealer could get financing like we had. One of the reasons why was that back then, Harrel signed full recourse notes on all the deals. In essence, this constituted two approvals. If Harrel thought customers didn't have good credit or weren't trustworthy enough to make monthly payments, he wouldn't sell homes to them. He tried to protect the banks on the financing as well as himself. That was where the recourse came in."

At one time, Cohron Homes had millions of dollars of recourse paper. Had things taken a turn for the worse, it could have been very tough for the company. Thankfully, it all went according to plan, and everything, in the end, turned out great.

It probably helped, too, that when the Cohrons and their

sales staff got off of work at 9:00 p.m., they would take the bankers out and wine and dine them until midnight or one in the morning. "Harrel didn't mind us going out," Woody recalls, "but we couldn't get so bad that we couldn't work the next day. He expected all of us to give one hundred percent."

And all of them did, to the point where the salesmen would work all day and then go out and look at trades after the work-day ended. "It was a double-edged sword," says Woody now. "If I left during the day to go look at a home, I could miss out on two or three potential sales while I was gone. I wanted to be on the lot when the customers were there, so I did my running after hours. I went all over the place, within fifty or sixty miles, to look at trades. Sometimes I got home at midnight. But, I always showed up for work on time at seven-thirty the next morning."

All that hard work eventually won Cohron's Homes a great reputation in the Indianapolis area. Harrel and Darrel's ideals also led their business to become one of the most successful sales lots in the mobile-home industry: First, you never lie to a customer and second, after a sale, you give good customer ser-vice and follow up to make sure that the customer is satisfied.

"They weren't concerned with looking out for number one," Woody recalls. "They knew that we were all in this together."

Because everyone knew what a good business he ran, Harrel never had a problem hiring new salesmen when he needed to, and the company quickly expanded. "When I started selling," Woody remembers, "the Cohrons had one mobile-home park with two hundred spaces. Today they have six parks with eighteen hundred spaces. They keep ninety percent or better occupancy—and that's a good percentage. They get these numbers because the Cohrons maintain the parks themselves and because they charge a lot less rent than any mobile-home park in the state."

Thanks to these advantages, the Cohrons enjoy the same low turnover in their parks that they do with their company's employees: Many of their residents have lived in the same place for thirty years or more. Some folks have even bought or traded up for newer homes three or four times. Some families have been in the Cohron parks so long that their grown children are now buying homes and raising their own families in the same environments.

"Our parks are our big advantage," says Woody. "We only put what we sell in our parks. Some other dealers get upset because they can't sell a home to anyone who wants to live in one of our parks. But being able to create and maintain the parks was a big investment for the Cohrons. The only way to make it all worthwhile was to sell the homes and make profits that would help pay for the cost of development. Other dealers didn't want to take that risk."

Eventually, Harrel and Darrel's sons came to work in the family business, and Woody was very impressed to see that Harrel and Darrel did not spoil or coddle them. In fact, they were just as tough on them as they were on all the other employees—sometimes, even tougher. The Cohron brothers wanted their children to learn the right way to do business.

"One Saturday in particular, when we were quite busy, one of the sons, Brad, went to Ponderosa to meet some friends and eat lunch," Woody reminisces. "Usually, none of us ever took more than thirty minutes for lunch, but Brad was gone for about an hour. At that point, Harrel went up the road and found him—he walked right into the restaurant and yelled at him to get back to work, though I'm sure the terms he used were not so polite. Brad never took that long for lunch again—and still tells that story to this day."

There are a lot of other stories about Harrel and Darrel's boys, too. Harrel ran the sales and financing end of the operation and Darrel ran the service department's home setup and delivery, but their kids worked in either department, wherever their interests lay. Bobby, Darrel's son, used to work for the service department in the summer, while he was still in high school. One afternoon, he called in to the sales office and said that the crew was up on I-465, and a tire had come off a truck and gone through the bottom of the paper on the home it was delivering. In short, they needed a new tire.

"Darrel got the message," Woody goes on to explain, "and loaded the tire in his pickup and took it to them. The guys knew they were in trouble when they spotted his truck. When he got out, he whacked his son in the ribs, said a few choice words and told the guys that he never wanted a home to leave the lot until the lugs on the tires were checked at least twice. I guarantee you that his son, and the rest of the crew, never forgot to do that check again."

Darrel might have been a little bit hard-headed when it came to running his business, but he was a genius when it came to developing Cohron Homes' mobile-home parks. If they had just sold the homes without places to put them, the business would not have flourished as it did.

The Cohrons' manufactured-home parks are among the best in the state. People are proud to live in Cohron communities because they're not stereotypical trailer parks. The Cohrons believe in taking care of the residents as if they are part of the family and charge the lowest rent they can, compared to other parks in the area that are not nearly as nice.

And that's the bottom line, the secret to their success: They treat everyone like family. Woody definitely felt that way when he worked for them. "I usually said 'we' instead of 'the Cohrons' because those of us who worked with them for years feel like we're parts of the business. We take pride in it as well. We're all part of the Cohron team—and what a team it's always has been."

Cohron's Manufactured Home Communities had always owned the majority of the mobile-home parks on the east side of Indianapolis. Then, several years ago, a land developer slipped in and bought some of the acreage at Pendleton Pike and Mitthoeffer Road, and sought to zone it for a new mobile-home park.

At the time, the Cohrons owned some vacant ground behind the sales lot, next to one of the new parks that we were in the process of filling. Darrel put the vacant ground up for zoning, figuring that he would send it for approval at the same time the developer sent the other ground. If the zoning board turned us down, he surmised, it would have to turn down the land developer as well—or, it would have to approve both.

Well, as it turned out, both areas were zoned for new mobile-home parks. Woody remembers very clearly the day when Darrel got this news. "He came into the sales office and called the land developer, and asked him if he wanted to sell his piece of ground. The developer said 'no,' so Darrel asked him if he objected to making a million-dollar profit on it. The guy said he would call Darrel back."

The developer did call back, and he told Darrel that if the Cohrons would pay the taxes on the profit, he would sell the land to them. Not long after, Darrel personally delivered to him a check for $500,000.

This was a risk for the Cohron business, but it panned out. In fact, it ended up being one of the best business decisions Darrel ever made. The park had no debt on it when he bought it, and he and Harrel were able to sell 400 new homes in it, and they made profits on all of them. To this day, it stays full; Cohron Homes makes the lot's rent every month. In the long run, it was a genius maneuver on Darrel's part.

Darrel and Harrel have had such a successful business partly because of the decisions they've made, either by themselves or together—though most of the time, they collaborate. Because of their proven track record, their employees have always trusted their decisions, even when they seem a little bit over the top.

Woody recalls just such a time, when, just after Cohron Homes had acquired that park from the developer, Harrel and Darrel called the salesmen together.

"For this to work," Darrel announced, "we all have to sacrifice a little. For every home that goes into that park, each salesman will put five hundred dollars of his commission toward park development."

"That seems like a lot," Woody explains, "but without the park, there would be no sales, so the sacrifice really wasn't that large. It all worked out. It all made sense."

And that was one of the things the Cohron brothers were known for: common sense. Using it, they were able to make decisions that brought their company—and everyone who worked for it—unparalleled success.

———

Before Woody went to work at Cohron's Manufactured Home Communities, he sat on the board of directors for several different credit union companies, and he learned they weren't all run the same. Some were very formal, with proper voting and minutes and agendas; some were more casual, with shows of hands and lively, informal discussions. None of them, however, prepared him for the board meetings run by Harrel and Darrel.

"Their board of director meetings consisted of the two of them throwing rocks at each other on the back of the lot," Woody says. "Or, through the wall in the back office, you could hear them knocking each other around."

Even as business partners, the brothers didn't always see eye to eye—but they never carried grudges against one another. Wrasslin' a little was just how they settled their disagreements. In the end, they always accepted each other's views.

"They could have their disagreements, but I guarantee you that they always have and always will love and respect each other," says Woody. "Nobody better ever badmouth either one in front of the other, or that person will surely be in for a fight."

As much as they stick up for each other, however, Harrel and Darrel certainly have their differences. For instance, whereas Harrel can fill out forms and attend meetings all day and all night, Darrel has never been one for paperwork or committees. Years ago, he was elected president of a mobile-home association; the very next morning he went into the office and had the secretary send the association a letter of resignation.

"That was probably the shortest term of office in the history of the mobile-home association," says Woody. "But it's also a great example of being true to yourself, which Darrel always is."

Darrel has also been a very fun-loving sort of guy, as is his brother—and anyone who works for them. A sense of humor is pretty much a requirement for working at Cohron Homes, as Woody can attest.

"Having a little fun is a big part of life there. People are always up to something crazy at Cohron's. Years ago, I had a little fun with the guys by bringing them an unexpected present: a huge statue of a cow. A local sign company had had it sitting on their lot for six months, so on a whim one day, I stopped in to ask if they would sell it. They did, for six hundred dollars. I brought it back to the lot and we put it out front as a stunt, just to get some publicity. Then, we made it into a permanent sign. There's no connection between cows and Cohron's, but everybody knows where our sales lot is thanks to that big ol' cow. We even paint it every year with the colors of the Indiana Pacers or the Indianapolis Colts."

In recent years, Harrel and Darrel's three sons have taken over ownership of Cohron's Manufactured Home Communities and just like their dads, they are dedicated to running the business with the Cohron ideals in mind. Sometimes, when a second generation takes over, a business can go downhill, but that is not to be the fate of this company.

Maintaining all the good business practices that made the company the success it is today, the sons continue to innovate in their fathers' footsteps and are always on the lookout for something newer and better. At one point, they had the foresight to start their own finance company and now finance about seventy-five percent of the homes they sell. Woody believes that in time, they will finance all of them.

Quite recently, the third generation of Cohrons has come into the company, and they show a lot of promise.

"It's exciting and affirming that the business still thrives," says Woody, "and I'm proud to have been a part of it."

Chapter 4

To paraphrase an old adage, you can take a boy out of Kentucky, but you can't take Kentucky out of the boy. Harrel and Darrel loved their childhood years in Butler County and to this day claim that their happiest times were there, in the carefree days of their youth.

However, those times were not always completely idyllic. When they were just two years old, their father died, leaving their mother to raise the family and keep the farm all by herself. Consequently, she did not have time to sit and play with or read stories to the twins. She had enough on her hands just making sure they survived.

Still, both Harrel and Darrel remember their mother fondly. They were too young to know their father before he passed away, so their mother was really the only parent they ever knew, and they were close to her. A large, heavyset woman who was very loving and very affectionate, they remember her simply as a wonderful woman and a wonderful mother.

However, their time with her was also, sadly, quite limited. Harrel and Darrel's mother passed away when they were ten.

Still, though they had hardships to endure and not much in the material sense, they had fun, and their lives were full.

They enjoyed each other's company and spending special days like Christmas together; their sister, Dean, recalls simple traditions like stringing popcorn and cranberries to use as garland on the tree. They would also cut pretty pictures from magazines and the Sears & Roebuck catalog and use the foil wrappers from chewing gum to make paper chains and other decorations.

Harrel and Darrel recall being friends with families such as the Guthys, the Millers, the Youngs and the Bashams, all of whom lived in their neighborhood. They also remember going on a vacation with some neighbors when they were ten or eleven, to the Barron River, where they set out lines for trout. Harrel and Darrel have always loved fishing; it's still a favorite pastime that they have enjoyed with their children, grandchildren and great-grandchildren.

As children, of course, the boys always looked forward to the weekend, when, according to Harrel, they regularly attended church and Sunday school. They also played ball and lots of homemade games, rolled tires, worked and went hunting and fishing.

The twins attended the Little Muddy Church and School in Butler County, though it was never one of their favorite pastimes. They were smart and clever, but school work didn't hold their attention. Their grades were mediocre—good enough to get by, but nothing to rave about.

Darrel has said, only half jokingly, that all a person really needs is a third-grade education. "If you're lazy, then you need a good education. If you're a hard worker, you don't need it."

He also says—with a wink—that he was the valedictorian at the University of Little Muddy. In the next breath, he'll admit, "Hell no, I just made that up."

Some children have career aspirations early on; some seem to be born with a clear idea of what they want to do when they grow up. Some, however, have no idea at all and Harrel fell into this category.

"I had no idea what my adult life would be like," he states. "I didn't know what I wanted to do. I thought maybe I would become a farmer. We lived on a farm, and my father had been a farmer. It made sense to me that farming could be a part of my future."

On the contrary, Darrel states, "I always knew that I wanted to be in business. But, I had no idea about what form of business or what I would like to do. "

Even though he claims to have had no interest in that direction, Harrel showed signs of being a businessman as well pretty early in his life. Sarah Dean recounts that at about age thirteen, he was always coming up with ways to earn money.

"Hey, Darrel," he would say, according to Dean. "I know how we can make some money."

Darrel would eagerly reply, "Oh yeah? How?"

And then, Dean says, the boys would plot together. Harrel would say, "Let's do this…" And Darrel's reply was always, "Okay, okay, okay!"

Harrel and Darrel were just little boys when Dean got married. Her husband, Walter, was sort of a father figure to the twins as well as their older brother, Paul. Walter enjoyed watching them wrestle and would give a nickel to the winner. Always clever, Harrel and Darrel would both fall down at the same time so Walter would declare them both the victor and give them each a nickel.

Dean laughs at this memory. "It was ten cents more than he really had," she said. "But he loved those boys as much as he loved our own daughters."

Harrel and Darrel agree that Dean and Walter had a huge impact on their lives. "Walter was a great hunter and fisher," Darrel says. "He was awfully good to us."

The Cohron twins are also indebted to older brother, Paul, for helping to raise them along with Dean after their mother died. They credit Paul with instilling them with the work ethic that still motivates them today, and they are forever grateful for the love and guidance of their siblings.

———

In 1939, Dean and Walter moved to Indiana because there was no work for them in Kentucky. They lived in a tiny, one-room house. Dean worked at a laundry service for twenty-four cents an hour and Walter earned fifty cents an hour loading boxcars with fertilizer. After the death of her mother in 1942, Dean and Walter returned to Kentucky to help take care of Harrel and Darrel. They stayed until Paul got married in 1943 and the twins went to live with him and his wife, Mary, in another area of Kentucky.

When Dean returned to Indianapolis, she worked as

a riveter in an airplane plant—think Rosie the riveter. She enjoyed the job, and was thankful to have steady work. But then, in an instant, it was over; she recalls the moment as if it happened yesterday: "We got the announcement that the Japanese had surrendered. Two hours later, the plant closed. Just like that. We were told to take our tools and go home."

Though she remained in Indianapolis, she always went to visit Harrel and Darrel when she could, and they always looked forward to her visits. "I put presents for them on layaway," she recalls. "I would put down ten cents a week. Those two boys would wait up for me to get there, to see what I would bring them. I would also bring big sacks of bread from the Wonder bakery and Red Cross macaroni. Six or eight big boxes. It was a treat. They ate off the farm, so anything different like that was real special."

She also recalls getting letters from Paul, saying that Harrel and Darrel were not attending school. They were rambunctious teenage boys by then, and Paul and Mary had children of their own. Together, Paul and Dean and their spouses decided that it was time for the twins to move to Indianapolis.

In 1948, Harrel and Darrel Cohron moved to Indianapolis, where they lived in Dean and Walter's garage. They stayed there throughout their high school years, which they both enjoyed greatly. They had a lot of friends and a lot of fun at Warren Central High, and they were always very active, playing football and holding down jobs that included setting bowling pins at Pritchard Hund O'Grady Bowling Alley on Washington Street in Indianapolis.

However, they were not always so carefree. Sometimes, they could be downright serious. While still a student, Harrel volunteered to join the military with a friend. He felt the desire to serve his country—but Dean was devastated by the thought of it.

Darrel, too, did not want him to go. "Don't sign the papers," he said. But Harrel was insistent; his mind was made up.

There was only one problem: Because Harrel was a student, he needed permission from his guardian to enlist. Dean says that they all went back and forth about it for a long time, and they all bawled their eyes out. In the end, brother Leonard, who was Harrel's legal guardian, would not sign the papers.

When he learned of this, Harrel went to Dean and announced, "Stop crying. I'm not going anywhere."

And then, the boys were back to their normal selves. Their prankster ways were evident even back then. Dean recalls their graduation party, a big picnic for which she fried eight chickens and made a heap of potato salad. Afterwards, the young grads took off for a joy ride and to attend other parties with their friends.

A neighbor later told Dean about the disappearance of a bunch of bras and panties off the neighbor's clothesline that night. Dean knew nothing of there whereabouts—until years later, when she found a pile of pretty undies in her cedar chest.

In 1953, Harrel got his wish in a roundabout way—he and Darrel were drafted into the Army. Knowing that there was nothing she could to about it this, time, Dean resigned herself to the fact that they would be leaving. However, she still wanted to have her say.

One afternoon, she marched herself into the Army recruiting station. She did not plan to contest the boys' being drafted; she knew that was set in stone. Instead, her plea was to keep Harrel and Darrel in the same unit. They had been inseparable their entire lives, and she could not imagine them having to be apart. For their sake and her own peace of mind, she asked the Army official at the local office to ensure that they would remain in the same order.

Surprisingly, the man agreed to it, though he did assert that if they had to go into battle, they would probably be separated. It wasn't exactly the answer she'd wanted, but it would have to do.

In the time leading up to the boys' departure, Dean was beside herself with worry. "My world was going to end when they left," she says, and she kept a fearful count of the days until they would be gone.

However, fate stepped in, and on the day Harrel and Darrel were to ship out, the war ended. They were actually on the ship already when an announcement came across the PA system that a truce had been signed with North Korea. They immediately received a new assignment: They would spend eighteen months in Tokyo, Japan, instead.

For the first part of their enlistment period, Harrel and

Darrel were stationed at Camp Attebury for training. They were allowed to come home every weekend. Dean still had her little three-room house and the boys stayed in the garage. To Dean, it sort of felt like they were just away at camp during the week. This arrangement went on until they were finally shipped out.

Darrel and Harrel served in the Army from 1953 to 1955, during which time they managed to live up to their old prankster nature. Once, Darrel had a weekend pass to go into town, and a buddy wanted it. So, Darrel let him use it. The friend was caught, and Darrel got in trouble. He was put on KP duty—which, ironically, he ended up liking. He actually became a good cook while serving in the Army.

Harrel enjoys cooking, too, just about as much as he enjoys eating. However, to this day, there is one dish he will not eat: spaghetti. While out to sea on an Army ship during a rough storm, the troops were given spaghetti as their evening meal, and needless to say, sea sickness and spaghetti are a nasty combination. Harrel was alright, but some of the men around him were suffering, and one of them threw up right on his lap. Needless to say, that ended his interest in spaghetti.

Though both Harrel and Darrel remained in Indianapolis after their stint in the Army was over—and still live there to this day—they both continued to love farm life. Over time, as money allowed, Darrel bought a farm to enjoy on weekends and vacations. Harrel, too, bought farm land for hunting and fishing. Even now, Darrel says that he and Harrel work so well together because of growing up on the farm.

"On a farm, if something needs to be done, you just do it," he says. "And you love it. If the pigs get out, you just go and get them back in the fence. That's how Harrel and I have always worked. We've always been partners, since day one. We don't know anything different. We don't have an agreement on paper. We never counted hours or debated who worked harder. We both know that we're dedicated to the business and to each other and to our families. If something needs to be done, we will do it. Our motto is get up early, stay late, tell the truth."

Chapter 5

Harrel and Darrel played up their twin status to the hilt. As young boys, they enjoyed trying to switch identities to fool people, and they could always wheedle out of a situation by saying, "That wasn't me. It must have been my brother who promised you that." Even as adults, in their dealings with customers or suppliers, they have taken advantage of their identical looks.

Darrel recounts one tale that still makes him chuckle. "When Harrel and I first started our company, I always kept an eye on the parks. We had rules, and we expected our residents to obey them. It made life better for everybody.

"One of our rules was that we did not allow big dogs. It was stated in black and white in the agreement that every resident signed. There is a weight limit. But, there was one guy who had a dog that was breaking the rules, and we warned him and warned him that he had to take care of it. He always said he would, and we left it at that.

"Well, I was driving through the park one day and I saw this big dog outside the guy's trailer, so I stopped to have a chat with the man. I chewed him out, and it really pissed him off. When I left, he decided to take off after me.

"But, instead of following me, he saw Harrel driving to the dentist and followed him. When Harrel got out of his vehicle, the guy laid into him: 'You don't ever talk to me that way, you SOB, I'll whip your ass.' Of course, Harrel had no idea what he was talking about. He tried to tell the guy that it must have been his twin brother he had dealt with but the guy was so mad, he wouldn't listen to a word Harrel said. He wanted to punch Harrel's lights out.

"'Don't pull that shit with me!' the guy screamed. 'You can't fool me, I know it was you!' But it wasn't me, it was Darrel!"

Though that instance was simply a case of mistaken identity, Harrel and Darrel were notorious for pulling similar pranks to confuse people. Once, they even shared a driver's license. One version of the story says that one brother lost his driving privileges due to speeding and simply borrowed his twin's license. The way Dean tells it, the boys shared a billfold and one driver's license because it cost a dollar to get a license, and they didn't want to spend the money.

Harrel and Darrel often fooled their teachers and neighbors by claiming to be one another. As they got older, they also supposedly like to pick up each other's dates. One such occasion was not a plot nor a ploy—but it was destiny.

Harrel was set to go on a blind date with a gal named Shirley. However, he had a chance to be on television, on a mobile-home show. He told Darrel about the situation.

"You mean that little redhead Shirley?" Darrel replied. "I'll take her out."

So, Darrel picked her up and the rest, as they say, is history.

Darrel had a hunch right from the start that she was the one for him. "Once I met her, I just knew," he says. "You know that feeling that you get when you just know it's right?"

Darrel and Shirley started dating and have been married more than fifty years now. Harrel, ironically, married Shirley's best friend, Joan. The two women were close, and they were determined that the two of them would stick together. "That was more important than boyfriends," Joan says. "We always dated brothers or cousins."

About Joan, Harrel says he was attracted to her because "she was kind and clean and talked nice. I liked that she went to church, and I also liked that she didn't push it." Both brothers claim that they knew right away that these would be the women they would marry.

However, in 1955, Harrel and Darrel were both working at Indiana Bell, the local telephone company, while trying to launch their mobile-home business. When Harrel told his twin that he was going to marry Joan, Darrel told him, "You can't get married! You have a business to run!"

But with a baby on the way, Harrel and Joan were married in Zion Lutheran Church in New Palestine, Indiana, in September 1955. In August 1965, Darrel and Shirley were married at the Cumberland Baptist Church. Both had small, simple ceremonies—"short and sweet" is how they both remember them. There were not too many guests, just family. But that was perfect, and exactly how they wanted them to be.

After Harrel's wedding, he took Joan to Ft. Lauderdale, Florida, for a week-long honeymoon in the sun. They both wanted to stay longer, but they could only be gone a week because Harrel had to get back to his job at the phone company.

The next year, when it was honeymoon time for Darrel and Shirley, they, too, went to Florida for a week—to Daytona Beach. Darrel recalls, "It was our honeymoon, but Shirley cried because she was homesick!"

Since then, both Cohron brothers have returned to Florida many times with their families over the years.

Harrel and Darrel were always hard workers, and when they were both newly married, they found themselves dedicating a large portion of their time to their mobile-home business instead of to their young wives and new families. The brothers both recall feeling guilty that first year.

"Our wives cried every night," Darrel recalls, "because we were working too many hours. They wanted us home, and we were always working."

Still, they all say that they would not have changed a thing. Sure, times were tough, but that was life—that was normal.

During those first days, Joan worked at Western Electric and Shirley worked as a waitress as Buckley's Restaurant. With Harrel and Darrel's jobs at Indiana Bell, their annual incomes came to about $3,000. Harrel recalls that getting used to being married was more about getting used to being on a schedule and having to be certain places at certain times. Sometimes, he admits, he did not feel as though he had really been prepared to get married, but still, he would not have waited any longer to go through with it.

When asked for a piece of advice to give someone considering marriage, Harrel responsed, "Make damn sure you love her. She is a part of you." When it comes to choosing mates, we can't really choose who we fall for. It just happens, and that is the beauty of love. However, to make a marriage last and to create a strong union, Harrel proclaims, it is all about give and take. He says that it is not wise to argue, and that the bottom line in a lasting relationship is to make sure that you have things in common with your spouse.

Although both Cohron couples had their first babies almost immediately after marrying, Harrel originally thought that he didn't want any children. It was not his plan to have kids—which is surprising, coming from a man who had many siblings and identical twin to whom he is incredibly close. On the other hand, Darrel always wanted children—lots of them. He even says now that he would have had more if Shirley had been willing.

These days, Harrel and Darrel are both devoted husbands and fathers. Harrel and Joan had three kids, Bill, Brad and Karen, and Darrel and Shirley had two, Sheila and Bobby.

The brothers started from humble roots in Kentucky and started small in Indy as well. When Darrel and Shirley were first married, they lived at 7501 E. Washington Street in the Hoosier Trailer Park, in an eight-foot-by-thirty-five-foot 1952 Spartan Mobile Home.

Harrel and Joan lived in a little house at 9622 Pendleton Pike, Indianapolis. The Cohron mobile-home business is still located on Pendleton Pike—actually, right across the street. Mingling family and business is the Cohron way; the brothers are natural businessmen and family men. Their company is as near and dear to their hearts as their children. Their family history and the business history are one and the same.

Chapter 6

When the Cohron twins started out in business in 1955, there was no way to predict that they would have the top mobile-home parks in the entire state of Indiana. But that success is a testament to their characters and their business acumen.

Today, they have six manufactured-home parks in the Lawrence area, in suburban Indianapolis: Briarwood, Briar Creek, Quail Creek, Post Acres, Parkwood and Greenbriar. Three of the parks are family oriented while the others are geared toward seniors and empty nesters.

All the parks have rules for the residents to abide by, to keep the communities safe, clean and neighborly. But the most important element in the success of these parks is the Cohron factor. As they always say, the most important things about our homes are the people who live in them.

For retired folks, single people or those starting families, the Cohrons have mobile-home parks to fit every need, budget and lifestyle. The parks are all in fairly close proximity to each other as well as the main sales lot, which makes maintenance and upkeep easy. This is good for the Cohron business and for the people who live in the parks. If there ever is a problem with any resident or with a home, the people know that help is just a quick phone call away, and that someone will be right out to look into it. Being nearby also means that the Cohrons can patrol their parks to make sure that everything is up to snuff.

For the uninitiated, some explanation on the term "mobile homes" might be worthwhile. Many people have in their minds dumpy trailer parks where the residents are less than clean and no one takes pride of ownership. The term "trailer trash" often comes to mind. That kind of mobile-home park does exist, but those places are light years away from the Cohron communities. The Cohrons wish that everyone could personally take a drive through one of their parks to see for themselves the levels of quality and care that make them wonderful places to live.

The Cohrons screen their residents to ensure that they will be a good fit for the communities, and they expect their homeowners to take as much pride in their houses as the Cohrons do. The relationships they form are mutually beneficial—the homeowners like living in places that are well kept, and the Cohron family likes to sell to folks who will maintain their homes. It's a win-win situation for all involved.

When it comes to the houses themselves, however, the words "mobile home" are a little misleading, as the homes are not at all moveable. Factory-built homes are delivered to the site on which they will reside, yes, but then they are installed on foundation piers, tied down with steel straps and anchors and made as permanent as any other kind of home. They are not trailers or temporary structures; they are the real deal. Nearly 2,000 families in the Lawrence area would agree.

Nowadays, they are more often called "manufactured homes," since that is a better representation of what they actually are, but the term "mobile home" seems to be sticking around nonetheless. At any rate, what they are called doesn't matter as long as people realize that they are not cheaply or poorly made. The manufactured homes that the Cohrons sell are top quality and surprisingly spacious, and options abound for their purchasers—laundry rooms, fireplaces, sun porches, you name it. A manufactured home can have all the high-quality amenities of and size comparable to a typical construction-built house but at a much lower cost, which accounts for their wide appeal in the Indianapolis area and across the country.

Manufactured homes are also quality built and sided, making the aesthetics of the Cohron communities pleasing, and the flowers and landscaping that the homeowners add make the neighborhoods additionally attractive. The roads throughout the parks are all paved, and the white-picket fences bordering the properties completes the look.

Even though he is retired, Darrel still enjoys spending his time out and about, cruising through the parks, talking with the residents and reminiscing about the good old days. Darrel remembers that he and his brother owe their success in mobile sales to a man who taught them early on how to sell: Mike Michaels.

Harrel recounts working at Mike's grocery store and trailer sales lot when they were just young men, before they were drafted into the Army.

"The pay was fifty cents an hour, but the lessons we learned were invaluable." He and Darrel were loyal to Mike and appreciate all that they learned under his guidance—including the solid work ethic and how to work with people.

Harrel and Darrel did everything during those days with Mike. He had fifteen lots and gave the young men a wide variety of odd jobs. Harrel even recalls cleaning out a meat cooler full of maggots—real character-building kinds of chores.

Harrel also remembers when someone stopped in the grocery store to ask for directions. The guy wanted to know how to get to Highway 40, but Harrel didn't know. Sadly, he sent the man back on his way with no clue where he was going. The next day, Harrel was mortified when he realized that Highway 40 and Washington Street, where the store was located, were the same road.

As far as Harrel and Darrel are concerned, Mike Michaels formed the path of their lives. He was a good teacher, and they were star students—and he sort of unwittingly ushered them into the mobile home business. The first home the Cohrons bought was simply a moneymaking deal, a quick flip for cash—a method that still works today. They bought a not-so-nice home, fixed it up and sold it for a nice price. It worked, and they did it again and again.

By the time they left for the Army, Harrel and Darrel had sold seven or eight mobile homes. Dean kept the money for them and when they returned home in 1955, they had $10,000 waiting for them.

Their first big purchases with that chunk of money really were no surprise. What would identical twin brothers buy?

Identical twin cars, of course. They each bought a 1955 Ford Victoria, though Harrel went with a brown-and-white model while Darrel chose blue and white.

Their second purchase was, though they didn't know it at the time, their first step toward the start of something truly big. With the rest of the money, they bought one acre containing a little, condemned house, located at 9622 Pendleton Pike—the location of Cohron Homes today—for $4,500 and a mobile home for $600. They put the mobile home up for sale in front of the old house and it sold for $800 plus a trade-in mobile home. They did a little work on that second home and then turned around and sold it for $800 as well.

With that, the light bulb went on, and the twins realized that maybe there was income potential for them in the mobile-home world.

But, being smart, they knew that steady work was needed even if a startup business was in the works. Both brothers ended up working at Indiana Bell until Harrel left in 1957, and Darrel followed in 1958. They left to begin their careers in the mobile-home business.

When asked if they would do it all again, choosing the same careers, they both responded, "Yes, exactly the same."

The 1950s was a good time for the brothers to get started in the mobile-home business. After making it through the Depression and then World War II, the nation was once again starting to blossom, and people were looking for utopia. Americans wanted affordable but beautiful, quality housing in nice, safe, convenient areas with good schools. This was particularly true for veterans, who could use the GI Bill to buy property with no down payment.

Based on these needs, America saw the rise of its first suburbs, modeled on the famous Levittown, Long Island. With industry in Indianapolis booming—farmland was being turned into factories, Western Electric, Chrysler and Ford moved in, and the US Army dedicated its finance center at Ft. Benjamin Harrison, which became the city's third-largest employer—The Cohron brothers saw their opportunity and began pursuing their mobile-home venture in earnest.

During their first year, Darrel and Harrel focused on selling used mobile homes. The secret to their early success was that they always paid as they went, so they had no debt. They didn't overextend themselves or bite off more than they could chew. They learned to take risks, but they were always educated risks.

As their business began to grow, the Cohrons knew that they needed space to make more sales, and they also knew that they had to focus on more than just new or used mobile homes. They needed to have mobile-home *parks*, too, if they wanted to make a go of it.

"Mobile homes have improved one thousand percent since we started in the nineteen fifties," Harrel states, though they always worked with the best materials they could find and top-quality dealers.

The first park that Harrel and Darrel developed was Post Acres, at 5135 North Post Road in Indianapolis. Formerly known as Smith's Trailer Place, it included twenty-two acres and thirty rundown homes on cinder streets.

This parcel of land was owned by a Mrs. Smith, who was going to give the park to her grandson, Clayton Cook—a fellow Harrel and Darrel knew from high school. However, Clayton was already busy working as a farmer at that time and had no interest in owning a mobile-home park. Always open to potential deals and new opportunities, Harrel and Darrel went in with Clayton and purchased a farm property in Hancock County for $40,000, which Clayton traded to the Cohrons for the mobile-home park in 1961.

In 1964, Harrel and Darrel started construction on the park, which needed a good deal of work. They decided to build two sections with 100 lots each to get started but also had to put all the utilities in place; there were no gas or sewer lines. In addition, the old, cinder roads had to be widened and paved. The total cost of the construction was $435,000.

At that point, the Cohrons also made a decision that still stands today: Residents of their community would have to purchase their mobile homes from the Cohrons. The homes could be new or refurbished, but they would have to come from Cohron's Mobile Homes regardless. And that ended up being the secret to their success.

The Cohrons' next venture was Greenbriar. Harrel and Darrel bought sixty acres at 9901 Pendleton Pike for $300,000 and developed this community over the following two years—which took a total of $.15 million to complete. The acreage was attractive to them because it was already zoned for a mobile-home park even though it was all farm land. Not having to fight for zoning was important. Even back then, some areas were strict about mobile homes because they wanted to limit their existence.

With Greenbriar, the Cohrons took what they had learned from the first park and included off-street parking for residents and guests. The community was developed in three sections, each with 100 lots. Greenbriar opened for business in 1967 and was filled to capacity within three years. One of the very first tenants lived there forty-two years—Mrs. Apple, who died just recently. Harrel and Darrel's older brother Leonard was employed as the property manager at Greenbriar for many years.

The Cohrons' third mobile-home park was called Parkwood, and it is located at 9300 Pendleton Pike in Indy. They purchased the lot for $280,000 in 1970 and began to develop it the following year. They also purchased another twenty acres from the local railroad company in order to make a retention pond.

The first sixty-five acre parcel included two houses and an apartment building in the downtown area, which Darrel and Harrel later traded to Casey Construction. As part of the deal, Casey did the development work on Parkwood. The Cohrons were always good at negotiating such barter arrangements, and they made great efforts to treat all of the contractors and subcontractors well.

In the late 1970s, zoning became an issue again. Some people thought that a mobile-home park would bring down the property value of their existing homes. This was not true, but because of these prevailing attitudes, Harrel and Darrel had a difficult time obtaining zoning for their next park. In order to get it passed, they had to obtain a variance and add it on to the existing Post Acres Mobile Home Park. The new park was an instant success. Before it even opened, they had eighteen homes sold and waiting to be delivered. The Cohrons finished the first section in 1976 and added sixty more lots in 1978.

The next parks were Briarwood and Quailcreek. In 1981, Harrel and Darrel purchased eighty acres at 52nd and Mitthoeffer for $400,000.

The next venture was Quailcreek. In 1988, Mann Properties had purchased the land where Quailcreek stands today and had obtained their zoning the same day that the Cohrons received zoning approval for Briarwood. Mann Properties had paid $6,000 per acre for Quailcreek, including zoning costs. Always looking to make a deal, the Cohrons called up Mann Properties to congratulate them on their recent acquisition— and to inquire about buying the newly zoned land. Mann claimed that they were not interested in making a deal. The owner and his wife had lived in a mobile home during the war and had loved it. They wanted to build a mobile-home park.

However, that dream did not become a reality for the Manns. In 1990, Harrel and Darrel purchased that sixty-five acres from them for $22,500 per acre. In 1991, construction began on Quailcreek Mobile Home Park, which had 380 lots in total. Between 1998 and 2000, the park was filled.

Over the years, the Cohrons have made other deals, though they did not result in more mobile-home parks. One time, Harrel and Darrel bought farmland but were not able to get zoning for a mobile-home park. It still turned out to be a great investment—they sold the property for double what they paid for it. They also bought a storage-unit business. Any savvy entrepreneur will tell you that the way to success is to have multiple streams of income. And Harrel and Darrel are savvy entrepreneurs.

Chapter 7

Throughout the years, Harrel and Darrel received a lot of support from the town of Lawrence and are grateful for the cooperation and respect.

"We could not have done it without Lawrence," Harrel states. The Cohrons quietly show their gratitude with regular and generous donations to the community's police and fire departments. They also do food drives and participate in various charity organizations. Their generosity is well known, but the folks in town will never know the full extent, as much of their giving is done anonymously. Harrel and Darrel simply want to help other people and do not need any recognition or fanfare in return. They feel that they have been blessed, and they simply like to share with others who need a helping hand.

And that attitude extends to the residents of their mobile-home parks. The Cohron family appreciates their customers, and they show it. Anything they can do to help the people who live in their homes, they will—starting with simply giving them a nice place to live. Drive through the mobile home parks and you will see well-kept roads, playgrounds and common areas. You will see lakes and white-picket fences. You will see mailbox areas with tasteful awnings bearing the reminder, "We love our residents."

That feeling is reciprocated. The residents of the Cohrons' parks really seem to like their landlords—evidenced by the fact that while their rents may be mailed in each month, many like to stop by the office and pay in person. They want to say hello and chat. And all the staff knows them by name.

The attitude of the Cohron family permeates all facets of the business. They don't put on an act just to make a sale. They are more interested in the long term, not just in what will make them a quick buck today.

Toward this end, they try to establish good, solid—and straightforward—relationships with all tenants as soon as they move in. That's why every person who purchases one of their homes and moves into one of their parks gets a packet of information laying out the rules, regulations and community policies are in a pleasant tone, like a friend would talk to a friend:

We have a list of rules and a lease for you to sign when you register. However, to keep it short and concise, if you can live with the following abbreviated rules, it will cover ninety percent of our community violations.

1. No large dogs are accepted when moving in, and sneaking large dogs in at a later time will not be tolerated.
2. One family per home, and anyone visiting in the home over two weeks must register with the community manager.

3. Keep grass mowed and trimmed on a regular basis. All trash and small-pet waste deposits must be picked up at all times.
4. Pay your rent on time. Late fees will be enforced to keep it fair for those who pay promptly.

Great places to live are made by great people. Use common sense and live by the golden rule: Do unto others as you would want them to do unto you.

The Cohrons' "do unto others" mindset has never changed, but their basic rules and regulations have adapted with the times. Back in 1981, they gave out this similar list of rules to their tenants.

These rules are believed by the management to be necessary in order to have a neat, clean and attractive mobile-home park and one that not only we but also the other residents of the community will be proud of.

Some of the rules:

- No loud parties will be allowed at any time, nor will loud radios or other excess noise be tolerated.
- Drunkenness or immoral conduct will not be tolerated.
- No peddling or soliciting.
- No go-karts.

- No drying lines for the drying of wash will be permitted on the lot. Umbrella type only.
- The speed limit in the park is 10 MPH. We ask that drivers use their brakes, not their horns.
- Only small one-half-ton trucks will be allowed in the park.
- Children are allowed in this park and must be protected at all times. Do not allow them to bother your neighbors.

Because they take care of their residents and as well as they take care of their company, Harrel and Darrel have built a multimillion-dollar business. However, they have never forgotten their humble, hardworking, farming background in Kentucky, and they have never forgotten to show their gratitude.

The Cohrons' work ethic and general attitude toward life has propelled them to be the number-one mobile-home business in Indiana and among the top one percent in the entire United States. Over the years, they have seen their competition come and go, but they've never been too concerned. They've had hundreds of hundreds of offers to buy their business, and they have always said "no."

Chapter 8

The minute you step into the Cohron office building, you'll see the sign on the wall: NO LOAFING, it states. It might be tongue in cheek, but it gets the point across. It makes everyone smile and keeps the brothers—and their employees—working hard at the same time.

"You can work hard and still have fun," Darrel maintains. "We're hard workers and we expect that of everyone who works for us. We also always expect them to know how to have a good laugh."

The staff at Cohron's Homes couldn't agree more. "We're always laughing and having a good time," says secretary Liz Riester. "We all know the value of hard work. Nothing is left undone and our customer service is unmatched. But wow, the antics that go on!"

During her first week of work at Cohron Homes, Liz wasn't exactly sure what she had gotten into—especially when she saw the local police taking Harrel away in handcuffs.

"It seems that these guys were always pulling practical jokes on each other and on their friends. Twenty years ago, it was a smaller town, too, and some things were easier to get away with. This particular day, if I remember right, Harrel or

Darrel and some of their pals had moved a truck belonging to Ray Cummings, their friend down the Pendleton Pike. Ray had known the Cohron twins for years.

"I'm not sure exactly how they moved his truck or where they put it. But Ray knew how to play their games. He had the boys from the sheriff's office come in and arrest Harrel because there was a report of a truck that had been stolen."

Liz laughs now, but at the time, she didn't know what to think. "Harrel, of course, always kept his sense of humor and kept his wits about him. I guess he knew that since he hadn't really stolen a truck, he wasn't really in trouble, so he had to get in a joke. As the police officers were taking him away, he said, 'Watch out for the gun in my pocket!' Well, that got them all riled up."

This initiation into the world of the Cohron family didn't shake Liz; she's stayed with Cohron Homes for twenty years and is grateful for her job—and for her friendship with the family. "They really do treat employees like family," she reports. "They've done so much for me, I cannot begin to tell you."

However, in the beginning, Liz wasn't so sure that she was going to make it—or that the company would, either. On her first day on the job, the company's accountant asked her to run a tally of the checkbook. As she did, her heart sunk. Confused by what she had found, she totaled up the figures again.

Liz says, "I could not believe it. I felt sick. I had just been downsized from my job at RCA, I was a single mom, and I needed a good job. I thought I had found one with the Cohrons, but after I ran the numbers in their checkbook, all I could say was, 'Oh, my gosh!' They were in the red to the tune of hundreds of thousands of dollars. I sat there thinking, *What have I done?* I have made the biggest mistake of my life."

Thinking that the brothers didn't even have the money to pay her a salary, Liz began to panic. The accountant came out to her desk and saw her distress. When she showed him the figures, however, he simply smiled at her and said, "Oh, the deposits haven't been recorded yet."

Needless to say, Liz reports that there has never been a dull moment at the Cohron Homes office. "Harrel was such a card. It was always a hoot working with him. He was the office brother and Darrel was the outside brother. I worked in the office, so I spent a lot of time with Harrel, and I love him dearly.

"He always jokes that he likes to copy stuff from other people, so he took the motto 'we love people' from a car-rental company. But the Cohrons certainly made it their own. They really do love people. They love their family and they treat all of us staff like family, too. They truly do love their residents as well. They sincerely care about the people who live in their mobile-home parks."

Liz also says that the big sign out in front on the sales lot that says "Cohrons' Manufactured Homes" was modeled after a cafeteria sign at a local restaurant that Harrel liked. "Imitation is flattery, right?" she says, "Anyway, it is a really nice sign."

Another longtime Cohron employee is Leroy Reynolds. He is much more subdued and quiet than the Cohron brothers, but they all have been great friends for about fifty years nonetheless.

"I started working with them in 1959," Leroy begins. "I've since retired, of course, but I owe so much to Harrel and Darrel Cohron."

Initially, Leroy hadn't come to the Cohrons looking for a job. In fact, *they* came across *him*. Harrel and Darrel originally met Leroy when they saw him hard at work. He was painting trailers, and his work ethic and talent were evident. The Cohrons understand and appreciate hard work and admire folks who take pride in what they do. Harrel and Darrel decided that they needed Leroy as part of their team, and so they hired him.

Leroy says that since that day, his relationship with the Cohrons has been amazing. "We've been friends for fifty years now. That kind of relationship doesn't seem to happen much in today's working world."

Recalling the early days on the job, though, he smiles at the memories of Harrel and Darrel's antics. "They were close, but they had their fights. I'd hear them hollering at each other. They would throw things. I'd just go have a cup of coffee and wait it out."

The Cohron twins didn't think anything of their little arguments or how they handled disagreements; to them, it was all just part of business as usual. And business always continued to get done—and grow and prosper.

Leroy was in charge of deliveries and setup. Sometimes, Cohron Homes was crazy busy. "I always worked from early in the morning to late at night," he recalls. "Some years, it was so busy, but we were glad to be busy. It was all a good thing."

Leroy can explain in detail how to haul a mobile home properly to the lot in the park and how to block it up. It is, of course, extremely important to set up the home correctly and securely, and Leroy and the crew ensured every step was done right. He was meticulous, and that was why Harrel and Darrel hired him in the first place. He knew how to get the job done right and took pride in his work. Every customer whose home was delivered and set up by Leroy expected and appreciated that kind of attention to detail.

However, it's not as simple as merely placing a mobile home on the lot. Besides blocking it up, securing it correctly and skirting it so it looks pretty, the water, sewer and electricity must be hooked up. Homeowners certainly want all of those things done right, and with Leroy, there was never any question that everything was taken care of.

Over the years, the demands of the job changed. Sales were not as high as in the early years and Leroy's focus shifted to the maintenance of the homes and parks. If there was a busted water line, Leroy was on it right away. Whatever the resident problem was, Leroy and his crew were there.

When Leroy recalls the years of his career with the Cohrons, he says, "They took a lot of chances, but they always seemed to work out. We did a lot at Fort Harrison in the early years. We were busy. I remember the crazy days of the business in the late

1950s and the 1960s. Harrel and Darrel weren't scared. They'd jump into things, but they always worked out for the best because of good timing and, I think, their attitudes. They're both very outgoing and have a lot of drive. They have their differences, but they've always made it work. Both of them have such good personalities and attitudes. There are no two better or friendlier guys than Harrel and Darrel Cohron."

Leroy ran the service department at Cohron Homes for many years; he also ran one of the mobile-home parks. He was the go-to guy for any kind of problem. He liked that all the Cohron mobile-home parks were kept up so well. It was a matter of pride to the Cohron family and the residents, and Leroy believes that the employees shared that pride—in their work and in being a part of the Cohron way of doing business.

"I always liked working for Harrel and Darrel," Leroy says, "and will always be grateful for all that they have done for me and my family. Their compassion is endless. They have helped me in so many ways. At one point they gave me a trailer to live in. They also helped out my sister when her house burned."

This depth of character in the brothers was well recognized by most people. "I always respected Harrel and Darrel. Always," says Leroy. "They could argue, sure. But they never held grudges. There was always total trust between them and they didn't question each other. They knew each other's strengths and respected each other."

And, of course, they had a lot of fun both on and off the job. Leroy enjoyed time away from work with the brothers as well. Hunting and fishing were two of their favorite pastimes, and they loved taking their friends along.

Leroy and Darrel hunted deer in Colorado every year. "We did it all," says Leroy, who sometimes went with them. "Those trips were fun for everyone. We would go fishing in Canada every year, too, up until Harrel got sick. Those hunting trips were something else. We took horses into the mountains. One year it was snowing so bad I didn't know if we were going to get out. We hunted elk and mule deer. We would drive back home with whatever we got. We would just throw the carcass in the back of the truck or van. Some years we had a motor home and we pulled a trailer in the back with the dead stuff piled up inside it."

Harrel and Darrel took their hunting pretty seriously—but always managed to get a couple of their signature pranks in along the way. Sometimes, after a successful hunting trip, they and the group of guys they were with would stop at a nice restaurant on the way home. Still clad in their hunting clothes, they would pull the truck loaded with their kills up to the front door and toss the keys to the valet.

Their sense of humor has always been their most-recognizable asset, but Leroy stresses that generosity is also a hallmark of the Cohrons. "They've helped out a lot of local companies all along the Pendleton Pike," he says, and it's true that the community has always been near and dear to their hearts. And, they like to show their appreciation for the success they have achieved.

"The Cohrons always did a big barn party every year before Christmas," says Leroy. "They still do. They were wild in the early days, when we were all young and drank and played cards. The whole community would come out. Harrel and Darrel like everybody, and everybody likes them. They are always up to something. This big old cow statue has been here out front of the sales lot for a long time, but they had a pink elephant out here at one point. It's always something, and it's always good and it's always a lot of fun."

That sums up life with the Cohrons, in business and in family and friendship.

Chapter 9

The Cohrons are open and honest, and that is the secret to their success in business and in life. They are all heart, but they also have great business minds. Throw in a zest for life and that is the winning combination that makes the Cohron brothers so unique.

Retired Cohron Homes employee Woody loved being a part of that—and he loves to tell the tales of their adventures. There were many, many over the years.

There was one incident at a restaurant in a Holiday Inn in Anderson. On the drive there, Harrel had seen a stray dog, a German shepherd, along the highway. Thinking the dog needed a home—and remembering how badly his kids wanted a dog—he picked it up and took it into his Cadillac. Since he couldn't take the dog into the restaurant, he left it in the car in the parking lot, with the windows cracked.

During the two hours that Harrel was inside eating, the dog destroyed that Cadillac. When Harrel returned, he could not believe what he saw. The dog had chewed off the entire dashboard and practically eaten the rest of the interior. When Harrel got back on the interstate, he left the dog there.

"I was afraid that he would eat me!" he told Woody.

It cost Harrel $2,000 to fix the car, and in the '60s that was a lot of money. The car had cost only $4,000 to begin with.

And, what did Darrel have to say to his brother about the whole incident? "I told you not to pick up that damn dog."

"It's funny," Woody says, "in more ways than one. He should have taken the dog in with him and let him destroy the hotel." He laughs. "We got banned from the Marriott, we could have gotten banned from the Holiday Inn, too."

No one will say exactly why the Marriott won't let them stay there anymore, but bringing ducks into the hotel during a mobile-home trade show and throwing the mattresses into the pool are just two stories that have been mentioned.

Woody has also mentioned one incident that happened in the private Learjet of a mobile-home manufacturer—Ray Bassett of Elkhart, Indiana. Harrel, Darrel and Woody all arrived at the airport with Ray in a black limo, and the driver ran them right up the runway—sort of like drag racing in a big, long car.

Once up in the air in the Learjet, they circled Notre Dame and buzzed the dome. Life is meant to be enjoyed and if you can get a ride in a Learjet, why not make the most of it?

But the Cohrons have never forsaken work for fun. In fact, they have mixed the two together. They can't imagine working without the element of fun. After all, there's no point to life if you're not enjoying it. Just like eating and drinking go together, so do working and laughing as far as the Cohrons are concerned. It really can be that simple.

All the Cohrons, not just Darrel and Harrel, share a love of life. Some of them, however, are more verbal about these feelings than others. According to Woody, Bobby, Darrel's son, and Brad, Harrel's son, who are keeping the honored family tradition alive these days, are the upfront Cohrons, the faces of the business now that Harrel and Darrel have retired. The other second-generation member of the Cohron Homes staff, however, belongs to the latter group: Bill, son of Harrel, who is rather on the quiet side, according to Woody.

Bill is a behind-the-scenes guy and because of that, he doesn't get the accolades that his brother and cousin do. As Woody notes, however, although he gets less praise, he deserves it just as much. "Bill is the unsung hero. He runs the service department and the parks. He is very low key and doesn't like attention or to be out in front. He's there early in the morning and stays 'til late at night. He might be a quiet Cohron, but he is a Cohron, and he has the same sense of duty and the same sense of fun. He's just a little less obvious."

Woody is not the only one who's noticed Bill's understated, unexpected personality. On Liz's most recent birthday, Bill came into the office and told her to close her eyes and hold out her hands. He told her, "Happy birthday!" and put a hand grenade in her palms. She loved it. She laughed all day and showed it to everyone who stopped in.

About the gift, Bill says, "We find all kinds of things when people move out of their mobile homes. This was the first time I ever found one of those things, though."

In the world of the Cohrons, every day is an opportunity— for fun, to help someone out and to work hard. That's how they look at life. They also expect the best from themselves, their staff and each other, and Harrel and Darrel never let their kids take the easy way out. They made them work just as hard or evern harder than everyone else.

Still, all the Cohron boys have their stories, their antics. Brad got hauled out of the Ponderosa for taking too long on his lunch break; Bobby got kicked by his dad for not making sure the lug nuts were tightened all the way; and Bill got fired. In fact, they all got fired at one time or another.

Bill recalls, "There was one time when I drove a trailer all the way back from somewhere, I don't even remember where at this point. I was only fifteen at the time. I got pulled over by the police, but they let me go. I assumed that was my scare for the day. I got all the way home and then, right there out front, turning into the sales lot, I turned too close and ripped the fence off. That was the first time that I got fired. That was just one of the times. There were more over the years."

Fortunately, these firings usually only lasted about a day. Whenever it happened, whomever it happened to learned his lesson.

With the other Cohron Homes staff, firings have been few and far between, probably because all the employees are so happy. The guys in the service department have claimed that working there was "better than working at Eli Lilly." And the shop guys say that anyone smart knows that Cohron Homes is a great employer.

The current crew has been around long enough that they worked under Darrel when he was the boss of the service department. One of the long-timers, Scott, says, "Darrel was great to work with. Buying lunch for us was no big deal to him. It kept us happy, fed, and back to work when he wanted us. We used to sell six hundred mobile homes a year. We delivered all over. There was always something going on. In later years, things slowed down and the deliveries were less often. Service of the homes became the main focus of our department. We responded to service calls right away, and whenever Darrel would see us sitting there at the shop, he'd say, 'Can't you dumbasses find a better place to loaf?'"

Darrel expected the best work from his employees because that was what he expected of himself. He pulled no punches. People always knew the score with Darrel. He never had any secrets, never did anything behind someone's back. With Darrel, it was all up front and out in the open—even raises.

As Scott explains, "We would all sit around the break table and get the word on our raises. 'You're getting paid this. You're getting paid this. You're getting paid this.' That was the way Darrel did it. And we didn't mind at all."

Woody agrees. "It is the same idea as how my salary worked. They laid it all out in the open. 'This is what you make. You sell it. You make the money.' And I made good money. So did Harrel and Darrel. Nobody there complained about the money they made or the benefits."

The Cohrons were generous, no doubt about that. Underneath their humor and silliness were real hearts and real substance.

Both of those qualities came into play when an unexpected

tragedy struck Cohron Homes. Woody worked closely with the another salesman, Lee Compton, with whom he had a standing ritual every Saturday: They had martinis after work. One Saturday evening, as Lee fixed himself a martini, he had a massive heart attack and fell over dead. Woody was devastated, and so were Harrel and Darrel. They were really shook up.

Brad recalls that at Lee's funeral, Harrel broke down and sobbed, which Brad had never seen before. He was very moved by watching his dad become so upset, and by Harrel's gesture of touching Lee's hand. Harrel and Darrel place a strong value on friendship, and their pain due to the loss was immense.

—————

Harrel and Darrel went above and beyond when it came to taking care of their people. Scott recalls a time when he wanted to buy a little fixer-upper house but the bank was giving him the runaround about a loan. That made Darrel angry, and he told Scott, "He's just a dumb ass. Tell him to f*** off and I'll give you the money."

As Scott puts it, "That was classic Darrel."

Harrel and Darrel were generous in all things, and especially when tipping. Woody says, "They were big tippers. I learned that from them. They were also big believers in business cards and always kept a stack of theirs on them. Always. Me, too."

Marketing strategies just came naturally to Harrel and Darrel; they made it look so simple. All they had to do, they figured, was be friendly with people and get their names out there. So, at every restaurant, they left their card and a big tip. They also tried to make as big an impression on the staff as they could. One of their most-used lines with the waitresses was, "Have you ever had sex in a mobile home? It's the best sex you'll ever have." The second-most used was, "You ever had sex in a mobile home? You want to?"

Chapter 10

The Cohron daughters, Karen and Sheila, are the apples of their daddies' eyes. And, both of them did their share of work at the Cohron family business. The girls did not have to be kicked or hauled out of restaurants; they were more concerned with hard work because they had been taught its value by their fathers. And, they have taught their own kids the Cohron work ethic as well.

Sheila says that all Cohrons genuinely like people and that this has been a big reason for the business' success. "Being around people is in our blood," she says. "Life has always been just full of people and fun and family. We never know anything else. We like to laugh. My dad instilled a sense of fun in all of us."

Sheila recalls her dad, Darrel, using fire trucks and dump trucks to water the plants at the mobile-home parks. He was an outdoorsy guy, and he did it all. Silly and whimsical genes are part of the Cohron makeup.

"Everyone knows us thanks to the great big cow out in the parking lot," Sheila adds. "At one time, there was a large, pink elephant with a martini in its trunk out there, too. Did that have anything to do with mobile-home sales? Of course not. But it was fun."

Sheila also reveals that her dad had a big, plaster elk in the driveway of his house—making it as easily identifiable as the Cohron Homes lot. However, she cautions that it shouldn't be confused with any of the game her father has brought home from his many hunting trips.

"My dad would take hunting trips out west every year. When I was very young I went hunting with my dad and Leroy but I did not take the big road trips with them. Those were certainly male bonding times. They would come back with dead animals and stories of their adventures. My dad has a big, black, bearskin rug at home that he brought back from out west. He told us that he killed the bear and we believed him for years. He was the mighty hunter, he always brought back stuff, so of course we believed him. It wasn't until the writing of this book that we learned he bought the bear rug off of some Indian in Arizona!"

Sheila says that although she did go hunting with her dad when she was young—an unusual activity for a young girl—there were some differences in how she was treated as compared to her brother, Bobby. For example, when she was sixteen, she wanted a car. Bobby had gotten a car when he was sixteen, so she figured that she should have one, too. However, their dad had the attitude that girls didn't get cars. Well, Sheila had other ideas—and loved the Bonneville she ended up getting.

The entrepreneurial spirit is inborn as well as nurtured in all Cohron generations. When Sheila was twelve years old, she wanted money for a new outfit. However, her dad would not just give her the money—he told he to earn it. They had a boat for sale, and it became Sheila's job to sell it. She did, and she got the money for the new clothes that she wanted.

Sheila remembers how much fun she and her family had not just in their daily life but on special occasions such as their boating weekends and their family trips to Florida. One time, they were on the way to pick up a new motor home in Iowa; the plan was to pick it up at the factory and then continue on with their vacation in it. However, when they arrived at Lifetime Motor Homes, they received the shock of their lives: Their motor home was nothing more than an engine, two boxes and a board with carpet. The company had not completed their order by the date that they'd said they would.

So, Darrel went down the road to the Winnebago dealer where bought a *different* new motor home. The whole family jumped in, and off they went to San Antonio for their vacation.

Problems like that notwithstanding, all the Cohrons' family trips were full of fun and adventure and good spirits. Sheila recalls, "One year, we were on a trip down to Florida and we made a sign for the window: "Florida or bust." In the middle of the trip, though, the motor home died. We watched it get towed away, still with our sign in it. I guess it was bust…or, rather, busted."

Sheila came from a generation of Cohrons that enjoyed childhoods that were a little more idyllic than Harrel's and Darrel's had been. In contrast to the twins' upbringing during the Depression in the rural South, Sheila explains, "I had a pony. A black Shetland pony named Blackie, of course. My cousin, Bill, and I played together a lot when we were growing up. We both loved horses. Uncle Harrel even had a little buggy. We spent a lot of time outdoors and had a lot of fun. It was a sad day when Blackie died. He was hit by a semi truck on the road near our property. We had other horses after that, though."

Sheila smiles when talking about her dad. "He never lost his love of farms and farm life," she says, and notes that he collects tractors. He's known for riding around in his Kubota, pulling a knee board and five little grandkids around the yard. However, he's also known for always getting stuck.

"He thinks he can do anything," says Sheila, "and he can, but he gets stuck a lot. It's become a running joke."

One time, Darrel went to an auction and bought yet another old tractor. Shirley always asked why he needed another. This time, he stuck a sign on this tractor and put it in the front yard. The sign read: "Divorce Sale."

Shirley got a phone call from someone who had driven by. "I didn't know you were getting divorced," this friend said.

"Neither did I," Shirley replied.

Shirley called Darrel, who had gone back to the sales lot, and asked him what was up.

"Well, it might be divorce soon if I don't sell some of my stuff." Darrel grinned. "I don't want you to get pissed."

According to Sheila, having signs made with various statements and putting them all over town for different practical joke situations was a favorite pastime of Darrel's. "The sign man loved him. We kept him in business," she joked.

Darrel is always getting into trouble, according to Sheila, especially since he bought some farm property about five years ago. "He thinks he and his Jeep are invincible. Well, he and his Jeep got stuck in the slough. I'm not sure what he was thinking when he tried to drive across it. Maybe just to prove that he could. Maybe he had a real reason, I don't really remember. I just remember that there he was. The water was coming in through the Jeep doors. He was stuck. The neighbor and his tractor had to come pull them out."

Darrel also has a garden and in the process of creating and maintaining it, has gotten stuck in the dirt many times. "That is the Fort Knox of gardens," Sheila reports. "The one-acre plot is completely fenced in now to keep out the deer and the rabbits and anything else that eats the vegetables."

Aside from tractors and gardening, Darrel has a variety of other hobbies. As Sheila says, he simply likes to collect things, and if he sees something he likes, he buys it. He has a big pole barn behind his house to hold all his "toys," as Sheila calls them. He loves to go to auctions and buy tractors or anything else that grabs his attention. Once, he even bought a covered wagon.

"It was an Amish-made wagon, absolutely beautiful," Sheila says. Darrel had it out one night and it started to roll down the slight incline from the driveway near the pole barn into the small pond on their property. As the covered wagon rolled, Darrel ran for a rope and tried to lasso it before it fell in and sank to the bottom of the pond. He hollered for Shirley, too, but she couldn't do anything to help, so she tried to call the grandkids.

Well, Sheila's sons, Kirk and Dustin, thought Grandma and Grandpa were just pulling their legs, as they always did—that Grandpa especially was being a trickster again. As Grandma Shirley begged for help, they simply laughed and hung up on her. They thought she was teasing; they had no idea that their grandpa was truly standing there with a rope tied to the covered wagon, using all his might to keep it from falling all the way in the pond.

Shirley called the boys back, however, and finally they realized that their grandpa really was fighting a literally sinking battle with his covered wagon. When Kirk and Dustin arrived at their grandparents' house, the headlights of Grandma Shirley's car were pointed at the pond and there was Grandpa Darrel, hanging on to the rope so the covered wagon would not become fully submerged.

Kirk and Dustin helped him pull it out of the water and back onto high, dry land. These days, it sits on the property of a local grade school.

Sheila and Bobby cherish the memories of their childhood and love that their kids get to enjoy the company of their father as well. Darrel adores all his children and grandchildren, and every year they take Christmas vacations together—all eleven of them.

"The memories of all those trips are unbelievable," says Sheila. "We went to Aruba and Hawaii, and we went on cruises. My dad likes the water as much as he likes his grandkids. We all say that he can float on the water on his back while he is asleep."

Granddaughter Mindee also has many fond memories of time spent with her grandparents on their yearly family vacations. One of her favorite stories is about a morning ritual they had during the summer, at Darrel and Shirley's lake house in Bloomington, Indiana.

"Growing up, we would go to the lake almost every weekend during the summer," Mindee recalls. "Every morning, my grandpa would be the first person up. My brother and I slept on the loft and my cousins in an adjoining room. Grandpa would wake us all up and we would come running, still in our pajamas, with our hair going every which direction. We would all pile into the car and go to the convenience store with Grandpa to get his paper and coffee.

"When we got there, he told all of us to get as much candy as we could hold—but before we got back in the car, he told us not to eat a piece of it until after we had the breakfast that Grandma was making for us. By the time we got back to the house, however, half of our candy would be gone, and our hands would be sticky. Grandpa would just laugh and act like he never heard any of the wrappers being opened."

Moments like those—which happened often, according to

Mindee—made it clear that Darrel and Shirley's five grandchildren were their favorite people in the world.

The Cohron clan has done the occasional winter vacation as well—it hasn't been all boating and fun in the sun. They've gone skiing, and Sheila remembers her dad on skis. She can picture the day and the big Caterpillar hat on his head.

"He wiped out and took four people with him," she says with a laugh. "One of the guys taken down said, 'Mister, you can maybe drive a Cat, but you sure cannot control those skis.'"

Vacations, of course, were among the high points of Sheila's childhood, but the stuff of everyday life was always fun, too. "We had baby rabbits and baby coons as kids," she says. "My dad bought baby ducks and baby rabbits for Easter gifts for the grandkids. There was never a dull moment!"

Later on, when Sheila had her own kids, Darrel enjoyed teaching all of them how to drive. Dustin prides himself on the fact that when he was only thirteen, his grandpa let him drive all the way to Bloomington. The Cohrons are a hands-on, active, involved family. Darrel and Harrel are very much a part of their kids' and grandkids' lives. They can't imagine it any other way.

And because of this, all of the offspring have some great Harrel and Darrel stories to tell. At many family get-togethers, all someone has to say is, "Remember when…?" And everyone will keep it on going from there.

Many stories involve the Cohrons' love of hunting. Besides being notorious for hunting on land too close to civilization—as in, right in town—Darrel and Harrel have always liked to discover unchartered territory, places where maybe there was a "no trespassing" sign. On one particular Thanksgiving, Harrel and Darrel and their sons went hunting and snuck onto some land. This, however, was not their lucky day. They got caught—or, at least, Bobby and Brad did. They were handcuffed and arrested and hauled away. But, instead of coming to their rescue, Harrel and Darrel pretended not to know them. This is one of those stories that gets told again and again and never grows old.

One of Sheila's favorite memories involves her dad trying to pay her off to stay home with him forever.

"When I told my father that I was going to get married," Sheila says, "he told me not to. He said, 'Don't do it!' He also told me he would pay me ten grand to stay at home with him. He took me down to Papa's Restaurant, and we had lunch and talked. He earnestly said he would give me ten thousand dollars if I would not go through with it."

Of course, Sheila did get married after all, and Darrel got over the blow of losing his only daughter—especially when she gave birth to a precious grandson. "All I had to do was have that grandson and all was well again," Sheila recalls.

Karen is the youngest of Harrel's three kids, and she is Daddy's girl. She always loved being a part of the business and was always proud to help out in any way possible. "When I was just ten years old, I loved to help clean around here," she states.

Karen also loved the residents in her family's mobile-home

parks, and felt like it was second nature for her to be there. In high school, she became a manager in the parks. It was a lot of responsibility, but she loved it.

"In 1983, I started as the manager at Briarwood. It was a new community and I worked hard to get it filled up. We all worked hard. And we don't just fill our parks with whomever. We take only good people. I love our residents just as much as my dad and Uncle Darrel do."

In 1988, the Cohrons were just getting Quail Creek started, so Karen went over there and became its manager, to get it going. "We filled up that one too, of course," she reports.

Karen cherishes the people skills that she learned from her dad and uncle. "They're Southern boys, so they were taught that you were always respect your elders and that you show respect for everyone. That is what we all were taught."

The Cohrons genuinely like people. "It helps to have a people-first attitude no matter what kind of business you're running," Karen says. "Our motto—"we love people"—is really true. We love our people."

Another thing that Harrel taught is daughter is that running a business means enforcing the rules. "The good residents respect that and expect that," says Karen. "They want to live in nice, safe, clean communities. We take pride in our mobile-home parks and we take pride in the people who live in them. My dad taught me that everyone deserves a second chance. There might be some kind of problem that comes up and you don't ignore it, you address it. You give a chance or two, but if there is a third time, you have to get them out. No one wants to live next to someone who does not return the care and respect that is expected of all our home owners."

Just as her siblings do, Karen insists that she had an enormous amount of fun while growing up. "There were so many good times—like summer camping at Lake Monroe. We started out with tents. Then, we got the pull-behind camper. Then, we got the Winnebago. We would go boating and skiing. We always had a blast."

Sometimes, Harrel and Darrel would take the camping trips with both their wives and all the kids together, and sometimes they would alternate weekends away. In the early days, they would not both leave the business alone for a weekend. One or the other of them was always there.

According to Karen, the family would sometimes be joined by friends of her dad and Uncle Darrel, including Karl and Fred. "We would go for weekends with them and their families. It was always so much fun. The adults would sit around and play cards and the kids would swim. My dad was always such a great example, showing us how to treat people and that you could have business with pleasure. He would not have it any other way!"

As the Cohron Homes employees themselves have mentioned, Karen asserts that the people who worked there together would all hang out together as well. "We had our trips as families and they had their trips as hunting buddies. Or fishing or whatever. Harrel and Darrel both like to keep people entertained and happy. Their whole lifestyle is about enjoying yourself and making life count. Since they lost both their parents at a young age, they know how precious life is and that it is meant to be enjoyed. That is why they loved their work so much, too. If you're going to spend that many hours doing something, you really should enjoy it or else what's the point?"

As far as Karen knows, her dad never lets anything get him down. "I remember one year when our family drove all the way across the country, to California, in a camper shell. By the time we got to Disneyland, both Brad and I had chicken pox!"

Many of the family vacations were to Florida. "We all loved going to Florida. And we always spent a lot of time driving around, checking out the mobile-home parks down there. They have so many people there who live in mobile homes, and those parks are gorgeous. We pattern our communities after the Florida-style mobile-home parks. They're beautiful places to live, there and here."

One of the most important things Karen's dad taught was how to enjoy my work and be a good worker. "When you see that sign out front in the office that says NO LOAFING, that is a silly and serious reminder. Hard work is expected. Giving your best is expected. My dad has always practiced what he preached. I remember there was one Sunday when I was a kid, and a resident in one of our parks called because their water main had broken. My dad went out there to take care of it. There he was in his suit, his church clothes, crawling under the trailer to fix the broken water pipe. People know that in a Cohron park, they will be taken care of."

In addition, Karen learned how to be tactful and honest by watching Harrel and Darrel in their dealings with people. "There was no reading between the lines with my dad or Uncle Darrel. It was straight shooting. They always taught us that when we say 'no,' we have to stand behind it and when we say 'yes,' meant you're making a promise. And we all learned growing up that when they Dad or Uncle Darrel said 'no,' you'd better not ask again. As a park manager, I have to say no a lot. I have learned how to do it tactfully yet strongly. I credit my dad for teaching me that."

For Karen, fond childhood memories are never far from the surface of her mind. "We were fortunate and blessed, certainly. But I didn't get everything just handed to me. I had to share a car with Brad when we teenagers. We had such great times growing up and now the grandkids get to experience how much fun it is to be a part of this family. Vacations are part of the tradition for this next generation now, too. Twenty-three years ago, my mom and dad started going down to Florida for a month every winter. Then they decided that a Christmas trip to Ft. Myers for all of us would be wonderful. They were right—it is wonderful. My parents, their kids and all the grandkids all together down there…that is really special. We always celebrate New Year's Eve together in a nice restaurant. It's a great way to end one year and to greet the new year. And, of course, my folks always still drive through the mobile-home parks down there to see what's new and what else is out there. It's good to get ideas. We always want to make our mobile homes the absolute best that they can be."

Karen thinks that Darrel and Harrel's success boils down to their good nature. "They give people the time of day. They listen. They make the time count and they are thankful for it."

Harrel and Darrel's mother,
Clyde Wiley Cohron.

Harrel and Darrel at about twelve
years old.

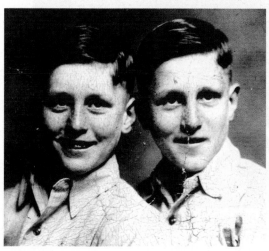

Harrel and Darrel before moving to Indianapolis.

The family around 1939: Dean, Clyde, Laurine, Paul, Leonard, Harrel and Darrel. Getty was in Alaska at this time.

Harrel and Darrel in Kentucky with their neighbors, who were also twins.

Harrel and Darrel with Paul and Mary and their daughter, Carolyn, in front of the old homestead right before they moved to Indianapolis.

Harrel and Darrel. High school years at Warren Central.

Harrel, Darrel and Shirley having a picnic. Joan took the picture.

Melodies Comm. 4 - Girls Concert Club
- Assistant 2, 3 -Operetta 2, 4 - Musical R?
view 3 - Melody Maids 3 - Choir 2, 3, 4
Madrigal 4 - District and State Solo and E?
semble Contest 2, 3, 4 - All State Chorus

CLARK, ELIZABETH - (Betty)
Sunshine 1 - Warrenettes 2, 3, 4 - Jr. Hon?
Society 2 - Accuracy Club 3 - Jr. RedCro?
3, 4 - News Bureau 2 - Kiwanis Award 3
Moods and Melodies Art Comm. 4 - Assist
ant 2

COHRON, DARREL
Drivers Club 4 - Future Farmers 3 - Moo?
and Melodies 1

COHRON, HARREL
Football 2 - Drivers Club 3, 4 - Assistant 3,
- Moods and Melodies 2

COLLINS, CARTER
Cross Country 1, 2 - Basketball 1, 2, 3 -Tra?
1, 2, 3, 4 - Future Farmers, Sec. 2, 3, 4
Drivers Club 4 - Alpha Hi-Y 3, 4 - Region?
Track 3, 4 - County Champion Track 3
Concert Club 1 - Beta Hi-Y 2

Yearbook photos.

Darrel and Harrel ready for the prom at Warren Central High School. They took Shirley and Joan as their dates.

Not sure if they were holding whiskey or syrup… They liked both!

DARREL C. COHRON 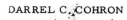 HARREL B. COHRON

Two of America's finest. They enjoyed their time in the military, where they learned they wanted to work for themselves. They didn't care much for being under the sergeant's orders.

U. S. NAVAL SHIP GENERAL SIMON B. BUCKNER

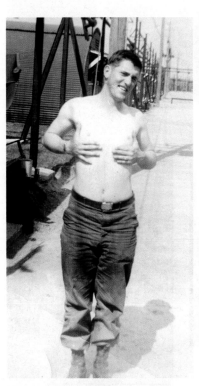

Harrel, Darrel and Shirley on a trip back to their homestead in Kentucky. Joan took the picture.

Joan in front of one of the first homes they sold.

First home sold.

Darrel and Shirley in front of their first home.

Leroy, Darrel and hunting buddies. Darrel came home from this trip with a bear rug.

Harrel and Darrel's first employee, Leroy. As you can see, he would do anything for them.

Harrel with Les Bell from Don-a-Bell Homes, 1956, at a show in Indianapolis.

An old sales order.

The cow in the original position on the sales lot, with a little trailer on a pole that was given to us by Holly Park Homes.

An invoice from Don-a-Bell Homes.

Construction bill while building Greenbrier.

One of Harrel and Darrel's first business cards.

One of Harrel and Darrel's early advertisements.

A view of Post Acres in the early days.

Darrel on a piece of literature from Holly Park Homes.

Cohrons' mobile home lot, parks flourish as others are bought out

By JEFF SWIATEK
STAR REAL ESTATE WRITER

THE COHRON brothers' mobile home park empire, 1,100 units in tight formation, is what co-owner Harrel Cohron likes to call "a neat and clean place."

Residents in the largest concentration of mobile homes in the Indianapolis area live by Cohron law — 40 rules that forbid large dogs, disallow more than two cars per home and require lawns to be in constant trim.

"Just live clean and normal — that's all I'm driving for," says the gruff-voiced Cohron.

Still, there's more to assembling the city's biggest holding of mobile homes than pushing neatness, even when mobile home parks have a public reputation of being dog-eared and a history of being shunned by communities that prefer site-built homes.

The Cohrons have combined neatness with a profitable strategy of filling their parks with homes that they sell and exploiting their parks' good location near the city's encircling beltway and Fort Benjamin Harrison.

Then there are the Cohron brothers themselves — identical twins who are a locally based exception at a time when most of the large central Indiana parks are institutionally owned.

HARREL and Darrel quit their jobs as cable splicers at Indiana Bell Telephone Co. to get on the factory-built bandwagon in the early 1950s, when it was just starting to roll. They had served as sergeants in the same Army unit in World War II.

Harrel tells how they chose the first Cohron's Mobile Home office, on a small lot across the street from their present sales office at 9622 Pendleton Pike: "Anything east of Post Road was $1,000 an acre; anything west of Post Road was $12,000. That's how we ended up on the east side of Post Road."

Today, the four adjoining Cohron's parks — Post Acres, Parkwood, Greenbriar and Briarwood — cover 200 acres, all in Lawrence.

A fifth park is under way, near Pendleton Pike and Mitthoeffer Road. Tentatively called Quail Creek, the 70-acre site will contain about 300 lots. It will open in August, at a cost of about $4 million.

The expansion will give Cohron's needed room. It has just 15 lots left to fill in its newest park, Briarwood, and an overall vacancy rate of 5 percent.

That's about half the city-wide average.

The new site already is zoned for mobile homes — courtesy of the seller — but Cohron's hasn't always had it so easy.

"We've had trouble zoning everything we've done," says Harrel. In recent years, Cohron's has encountered rejection of proposals for mobile home parks in Beech Grove, Warren Township and New Whiteland.

LAWRENCE has looked more kindly on Cohron's, although Lawrence has demanded greater investment in the parks' appearance.

At Briarwood and the new park, Cohron's must maintain a landscaped grassy median between the street and the first row of mobile homes. Homes in the first row are required to sport shingled roofs and siding; no home in the park may have a window air conditioner.

Cohron's also wins points from zoning officials by refusing, as a rule, to rent its lots for used homes. Moreover, if a shabby-looking home in one of its parks goes up for sale, the company tries to buy it for resale to

See COHRONS Page 3

Cohrons

★ Continued from Page 1

wholesalers in Kentucky and Arkansas, says Harrel.

"We could put an old unit in there, but it's not going to be increasing the value of our park," he says.

Letting in used homes also would cut into Cohran's own sales of mobile homes. It sold 125 homes last year, for prices ranging from $15,000 for a single-wide to $45,000 for a 28-foot double-wide.

There's a 10 percent discount for those who move their Cohron's home into a Cohron's park.

More than half of the residents in Cohron's parks are 55 or older. The company also discourages families with more than two children from moving in.

Retirees have filled the gap left by the dwindling number of Cohron's residents who work at Fort Benjamin Harrison. Less than 10 percent now work at the Army fort, compared to 30 percent in the 1960s.

AN ARMY-BUILT mobile home park charging below-market rents siphoned away much of the Cohrons' business, but the brothers don't allow feelings of unfair competition to get in the way of patriotism.

"Their pay's low and they deserve it," Harrel says about the low rents given to Fort Ben soldiers in the Army-run park. Cohron's rents range from $130 to $150 a month, while the Army charges less than half that, he says.

The twins, at age 55, figure to be around to see full lease-up of their latest park. Harrel's two sons, Bill and Brad, work as a service manager and salesman, respectively. Darrel's son Bob also is a salesman.

"I want to turn it over to them in the near future," says Harrel, who handles the company's home sales while Darrel oversees park management.

There's no talk of accepting any of the offers of purchase from institutional investors who've snapped up some of the area's largest parks over the past five years.

"It's just not for sale," says Harrel of his company's holdings.

He also vows loyalty to the landmark 14-foot fiberglass cow that stands in front of Cohron's Pendleton Pike offices.

Today's stress on curb appeal may prompt Cohron's to build two landscaped lakes at the entrance to its new park, but a huge cow, well, "I could spend $20,000 on a neon sign and it doesn't get me as much publicity as that cow does," Harrel says.

Article in the *Indianapolis Star and News*. Cohron's Mobile Homes sold eight homes the week this article was published.

Cohron's Mobile Homes leases park space to 1,100 mobile homes in Indianapolis. The wooden model belongs to co-owner Harrel Cohron.

STAR STAFF PHOTO/JERRY CLARK

Harrel joking with Fred Todd and Al from Schult Homes about developing new models for 1991.

Headstone of salesman Lee Compton. He loved the business and Harrel and Darrel loved him.

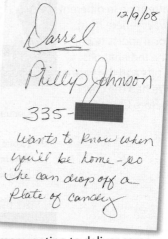

12/9/08

Darrel

Phillip Johnson

335-

Wants to know when you'll be home - so he can drop off a plate of candy

Note from a customer wanting to deliver some treats. Harrel and Darrel's customers are the best!

Business goes wild for its Wildcat hoopsters

Go Wildcats! Cohron's Manufactured Homes, 9623 Pendleton Pike, cheers the Lawrence North High School boys basketball team by painting its cow red and green. The Wildcats, led by center Greg Oden, played a perfect regular season (27-0) and is 5-0 in postseason play. The team has a No. 1 state and national ranking.

The Cohron's Mobile Homes cow gets attention in different ways—here from local sports teams the Indianapolis Colts and the Pacers. We had the cow before Chick-fil-A.

Billboard to commemorate Cohron's Mobile Homes' fiftieth anniversary and to thank the city of Lawrence.

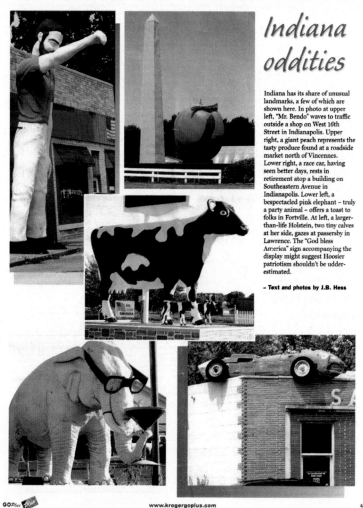

Indiana oddities

Indiana has its share of unusual landmarks, a few of which are shown here. In photo at upper left, "Mr. Bendo" waves to traffic outside a shop on West 16th Street in Indianapolis. Upper right, a giant peach represents the tasty produce found at a roadside market north of Vincennes. Lower right, a race car, having seen better days, rests in retirement atop a building on Southeastern Avenue in Indianapolis. Lower left, a bespectacled pink elephant – truly a party animal – offers a toast to folks in Fortville. At left, a larger-than-life Holstein, two tiny calves at her side, gazes at passersby in Lawrence. The "God bless America" sign accompanying the display might suggest Hoosier patriotism shouldn't be udder-estimated.

– Text and photos by J.B. Hess

The cow showed up in a magazine article on unusual landmarks.

SUBSCRIPTION AGREEMENT AND CALL OF MEETING

We, the undersigned, hereby agree to take and pay for the same, at their fixed consideration, the number of shares of the capital stock of

COHRON'S MOBILE HOMES, INC.

a corporation to be organized under the Indiana General Corporation Act of 1929 and Acts Amendatory, set opposite our respective signatures, said subscriptions to become due as soon as the organization of said company is completed. We hereby promise to pay the fixed consideration to the Treasurer of said Company on demand or at such times as the Board of Directors may determine.

Name	Address	Shares	Amount
Harrel B. Cohron, 9622 Pendleton Pike, Indianapolis, Ind.		49	490.00
Darrel C. Cohron, 9622 Pendleton Pike, Indianapolis, Ind.		49	490.00
Joan Cohron, 9622 Pendleton Pike, Indianapolis, Ind.		1	10.00
Shirley Cohron, 9622 Pendleton Pike, Indianapolis, Ind.		1	10.00

CALL OF MEETING OF SUBSCRIBERS TO THE CAPITAL STOCK OF

COHRON'S MOBILE HOMES, INC.

Indianapolis, Indiana   City
September 29, 1959   Date

Subscriptions to the capital stock of Cohron's Mobile Homes, Inc. a corporation to be organized under the laws of the State of Indiana, having been obtained in an amount not less than $1000.00 as shown by the instrument witnessing the same, the undersigned, Harrel B. Cohron Darrel B. Cohron , and Joan Cohron , the person or persons causing the foregoing subscription lists to be opened, hereby call a meeting of the subscribers therein listed for the purpose of designating the incorporators of Cohron's Mobile Homes, Inc. , electing the first Board of Directors to be named as such in the Articles of Incorporation of such corporation and determining upon, and executing Articles of Incorporation of such corporation, such meeting to be held at the office of 9622 Pendleton Pike, Indianapolis, Ind. , on the 29th day of September , 19 59, at 8:00 o'clock P.M.

Harrel B. Cohron

Darrel C. Cohron

Joan Cohron

Annual meeting commemorating the forming of the corporation.

AUTHENTICATION OF RECORD BOOK

The undersigned being the President, Secretary and all of the Directors of

COHRON'S MOBILE HOMES, INC.

a corporation duly organized and existing under and by virtue of the laws of the State of Indiana by virtue of the Certificate of Incorporation issued by the Secretary of State of Indiana under the great seal of the State of Indiana, on the 30th day of September A.D. 19 59, do hereby make and constitute this book as and for the record book of this corporation, in which shall be kept an accurate and complete record of all of its proceedings, including those relating to the election of its officers, proceedings of directors and shareholders meetings, the record of all shareholders from its organization showing the place of residence, amount of stock held, time of acquiring stock and time of transfer of stock; and the records so kept shall be and constitute the sole and exclusive evidence of such proceedings and who, as the owners of stock, have the right to receive dividends and to vote as such owners and who are liable for calls and assessments.

And for the purpose of identifying this record book, we have caused the corporate seal of this corporation to be affixed hereto.

Dated this 1st day of October   A.D. 19 59

Harrel B. Cohron
President and Director

Joan Cohron
Secretary and Director

Darrel C. Cohron
Director

Shirley Cohron
Director

(Corporate Seal)

Trip to Hawaii with Champion Homes back in the days when they wined and dined us.

Salesmen Jim Scott and Robert (Woody) Woodhouse conversing at Harrel and Darrel's annual Christmas party.

Bobby, Brad and construction workers at the start of Briarwood, around 1983.

Darrel surveying a lot at Post Acres.

Sheila, Darrel, Shirley, Bobby.

Darrel acting up.

Young Bob Cohron, ready to work.

Surprise fortieth birthday party.

October 1982, family reunion at Darrel's home: Getty, Dean, Paul, Leonard, Louise, Harrel and Darrel.

From the same reunion: spouses, "outlaws". Mary, Shirley, Walter, Jack, Laurine and Joan.

Harrel and Darrel at the annual cleaning and reunion at the cemetery where their mom, dad, and brothers Getty and Glen are buried.

Mr. and Mrs. Cohron

Mr. and Mrs. Harrel Cohron of Indianapolis will celebrate their 50th wedding anniversary with a trip to Mackinac Island, Mich., with their children and grandchildren.

Mr. Cohron and the former Joan Schwier were married Sept. 3, 1955, at Zion Lutheran Church in New Palestine.

Mr. Cohron was a co-founder of Cohron Mobile Homes.

Mrs. Cohron worked at Western Electric and then became a homemaker.

They are members of Servants of Christ Lutheran

Church on Oaklandon Road.

The couple has three children and seven grandchildren.

Darrel and Shirley.

Leroy Reynolds and his wife, Marsha, at one of Harrel and Darrel's Christmas parties.

Woody and Jim Scott at Christmas.

Darrel on a Parkwood Homes hunting trip.

Harrel and Darrel with brothers Leonard and Paul.

Harrel and Darrel and another set of twins at Karen's wedding.

Darrel, Dean, Paul (seated), Paul's wife, Mary, and Harrel. These are the family members who raised Harrel and Darrel after their parents' death.

Dean, Paul, Harrel, Darrel and their niece, Carolyn, in front of "Little Muddy"—the one-room schoolhouse Harrel and Darrel attended.

Darrel's farm.

Darrel with one of his hobbies: old tractors.

Company truck in the Lawrence Baseball opening day parade.

Harrel and Darrel with the sign in front of their school. They walked about a mile to attend.

Harrel, Joan, Shirley and Darrel.

Woody, Harrel, Darrel and Leroy at the Annual Strawberry Festival.

Bill Berkebile, Darrel, Woody, Leroy and Harrel (seated). Bill was a longtime friend from the Finance Center Federal Credit Union.

Darrel and Harrel at Christmas.

Harrel and Joan at Dave Burnside's home. Dave was a fellow mobile-home dealer and a neighbor at Harrel's lake home in Columbus, Indiana.

Darrel, Shirley, Dottie, Cleo Wilcher, Joan and Harrel. Darrel, Harrel and Cleo served in the Army together and became lifelong friends.

Shirley, Mike and Neva Michaels, Joan, Dean.

Harrel and Darrel receiving the Sagamore of the Wabash award at their sixtieth birthday party.

Surprise sixtieth birthday party. Mike and Neva made it in from California and really surprised Harrel and Darrel.

Darrel, Shirley and family.

Harrel with his grandchildren, 1996: Tammy holding Samantha, Jacob, Ashley, Lauren, Meghan and Travis.

Matt, Jenni, Darrel, Shirley, Joan and Harrel at Matt and Jenni's wedding.

Dean's birthday party.

Darrel at Okeechobee.

Good friends Karl and Jackie Theyssen. Karl handled all of Harrel and Darrel's heating and air conditioning needs over the years. He was a good fisherman, too!

Harrel, Bill and Terry Theyssen turkey hunting.

Harrel and Darrel with one of their deer conquests.

Harrel with his last big buck, killed on his farm in Jefferson County.

Reunion in the '90s.

Darrel and Shirley on the left, Harrel and Joan on the right. Taken after Darrel and Harrel both received a lifetime achievement award.

Bob, Sheila, Darrel, Harrel, Bill, Brad, Karen, Shirley and Joan at the lifetime achievement award dinner.

Sad degree of separation
Lawrence businessman hailed for his generosity, love of family

By John Tuohy
john.tuohy@indystar.com

Photos provided by the Cohron family

Twins Harrel (left) and Darrel Cohron operated Cohron Homes. Harrel died Dec. 30.

Neither Darrel Cohron or other surviving family members could tell who is who in this old Army photo. The brothers moved to Indianapolis from Kentucky in 1948. They were raised by an older brother after their parents died when they were young.

Identical twins Harrel and Darrel Cohron grew up in Kentucky together, moved to Indianapolis together and started a mobile home business together.

So when Darrel spent the last few days of Harrel's life lying beside him in bed, comforting his brother while cancer sapped his strength, it surprised no one.

"He was right there with him, sleeping in the same bed," said Brad Cohron, 48, Harrel Cohron's son. "He knew how sick he was."

Harrel Cohron, 76, died Dec. 30. But the local mobile home empire he and his brother built — Cohron Homes, of Lawrence — thrives, managed by second- and third-generation Cohrons.

"He loved this business. He met so many good and interesting people in his life," said Brad Cohron, who helps oversee the $8-million-a-year business which includes a showroom and six mobile home communities in Lawrence.

"Even after he got out of the day-to-day stuff, he was here every day, walking the grounds, visiting old friends."

Last Monday, about 1,000 people attended a memorial service for Harrel Cohron at Servants of Christ, the Lawrence church he helped found. Loved ones remembered him as an industrious but prank-loving businessman and outdoorsman whose own upbringing taught him the value of keeping family close.

Cohron's father died when he was 2, and his mother died when he was 10. He and his brother were raised by their older brother and his wife.

"He not only loved and cherished his family, he treated all his employees like family," said Lawrence City Council President Donald Poteat, who worked for Cohron Homes for 33 years.

Poteat said that when his own mother was ill in North Carolina years ago, Cohron, his boss, told him without hesitation to drive down south immediately and take care of her.

"And he said 'If you need some money, let me know,'" Poteat said. Another time, Harrel loaned Poteat money to buy a pickup truck after he ruined his car in a crash.

The Cohrons moved from Sugar Grove, Ky., to Indianapolis in 1948, and both brothers graduated from Warren Central High School in 1952. Right after high school, they bought a few shabby mobile homes, reconditioned them and sold them from the front yard of their sister, Sarah Dean.

By the time they left to serve in the Army in 1953, the Cohruns had sold about eight homes. When they returned in 1955, Dean gave them $10,000 that those homes had earned. With that nest egg, the brothers each bought a 1955 Ford Victoria — Harrel's was brown and white and Darrel's was blue and white — and a house on 1 acre at 9622 Pendleton Pike. They bought a mobile home for $600, sold it for $800, and soon they were in business for good.

Though Darrel Cohron was perceived as the more devilish brother — he used to scare neighbors by hunting rabbits in the vacant land around Pendleton Pike — Harrel had his fun side, too, Poteat said. Naturally, many of the jokes involved confusing friends and strangers about who was who.

Darrel Cohron said the differences in their personalities made a perfect fit for the business — the classic Mr. Inside and Mr. Outside arrangement.

"I liked to walk the grounds of the parks, and he liked it in the office, a born salesman," Darrel Cohron said Thursday. "We had our fights but they never lasted more than a couple days."

Harrel Cohron was an enthusiastic fisherman and hunter who owned a large property in Southern Indiana where he hunted deer. About a dozen mounted buck decorate the wall of his house there, Brad Cohron said.

"He has quite the collection," Brad Cohron said. "He even has a shark mounted that he caught in Florida."

It was to Florida that Harrel took his new bride, Joan Schwier, for their honeymoon in 1955. Darrel also took his wife, Shirley, who happened to be Joan's best friend, to Florida, on their honeymoon.

Lawrence Mayor Paul Ricketts, a longtime friend of the Cohrons', said they have been notable contributors to Lawrence's civic life for decades, donating to several police and fire causes.

He said the mobile home parks have served dual purposes, providing people with affordable housing and giving the city a solid tax base.

"They have been a great friend to the city," Ricketts said. The mayor honored Harrel Cohron with a proclamation at a City Council meeting Monday night.

Cohron is survived by his wife, Joan; sons, Bill and Brad; daughter, Karen; brothers, Darrel and Paul; sisters, Sarah Dean and Louise; and several grandchildren and great grandchildren.

★ Call Star reporter John Tuohy at (317) 444-6305.

Article in the paper about Harrel's death.

℘

102
J. P. Morgan's Wealth and God's Mercy

When the multimillionaire J. P. Morgan died, his will consisted of about 10,000 words and contained 37 articles. But we are left in no doubt as to what Mr. Morgan considered to be the most important affair in his whole life. He made many transactions, some affecting large sums of money. Yet there was evidently one transaction of supreme importance in Mr. Morgan's mind. Here is what he said: "I commit my soul into the hands of my Savior, in full confidence that, having redeemed and washed it in his most precious blood, he will present it faultless before my heavenly Father; and I entreat my children to maintain and defend, at all hazard and at any cost of personal sacrifice, the blessed doctrine of the complete atonement for sin through the blood of Jesus Christ, once offered, and through that alone."*

In the matter of his soul's eternal blessing, J. P. Morgan's vast wealth was powerless. He was as dependent upon mercy as was the dying thief at Calvary. He was dependent upon the mercy of God and the shed blood of Christ just as you too are dependent.

*Frederick Lewis Allen, *The Great Pierpont Morgan* (New York: Harper Collins, 1949).

℘

A quote Harrel kept in his desk.

Harrel in Arizona on a family trip.

January 17, 2009

Dear Joan, Darryl, Shirley & family;

Please forgive the typing rather than personal writing, but my carpal tunnel makes it difficult for me to write by hand.

I want to express our deep sorry for Harrel's passing. We know that is exactly what he did, pass on to Heaven into the arms of our Loving Lord Jesus. We just know he & Dad are there together & certainly laughing!

Even knowing he is in a much better place, I am certain loss you feel is unbearable & please know our hearts are heavy with yours & we pray the Lord will comfort each of you.

Darrel you have spent almost every minute, since conception with your Dear Brother & I know your loss must be tremendous. As brothers & twins you shared such a bond, I know your heart is broken.

Joan, your soul mate has gone on before you, I'm sure not having Harrel by your side is unbelievable at times. We pray for you & grieve with you. How great to have had such a wonderful husband for all those years.

Shirley, to loose such a great brother in law, how very sad. I love my brother in law as a brother, & your connection with Harrel & Darrel being twins, well, I know your bond was special.

While Patti & I were not able to spend a lot of time with you both, Harrel & Darrel, through the Love our parents felt for you, & you for them, in our hearts, we feel as you are our family, our Brothers back there in Indiana.

Who would have thought those twin boys Dad hired in his "trailer sales" would have grown up to be so successful in that business. Much more successful than Dad was, but what a great Dad he was! They provided us with all of our needs, taught us to be hard workers & most of all, taught us about the Lord. He & Mom were / are so proud of the fine Godly men you became & the business success you have enjoyed. Great husbands & fathers & grandfathers … Christians, …….. oh how they love you both.

How interesting it is that our Lord took Harrell on December 30th, & gave us a new Grandson, Kayl, on the very same day! Our youngest daughter Tricia & her husband Russell, had their first baby the late afternoon of December 30th. Truly, the Lord taketh & giveth.

Mom would like to talk to you more on the telephone, but she just can't hear well. She grieves along with you & really wants to talk to you Darrel. I am sure she will continue to call you & just please be patient with her, her lack of hearing & the dementia. I don't know if you have noticed, but Mom has become increasingly senile during the past few years. It is not constant & something we can deal with. She worries constantly that she has said or done something during her "bad moments" to offend someone. I hope that is not the case with any of you, but if she has said anything that seems strange or just different for Mom, or does in the future, please understand her condition & her age & forgive her. She loves you all so deeply.

Mom's health is good for her age, she'll be 91 in a little over 2 months. Her appetite is good, she pretty much runs on sugar! Mom is living with Charles & I & we hope to keep her here with us for many more years. She is able to see the grand kids & great grand kids very often. She manages to visit Patti & Steve occasionally, for a week or so at a time & is able to see those grand kids too. Mostly, she just stays home & enjoys her little dog, Sadie, a Maltese that loves her back.

Joan, thank you so very much for sending us the items from Harrel's funeral & the obituary. We have read & reread them. I sent copies to Patti's family also. Oh how touching they are. Each was obviously prepared with so much thought, caring & love. His funeral must have been exceptional. Even the Hymns, The Old Rugged Cross; Amazing Grace & Blessed Assurance. I could just hear Dad singing The Old Rugged Cross, one of his favorites & he would often sing it around the house. It made me think of Dad's favorite, In The Garden. I sang the The Old Rugged Cross in honor & memory of Harrel. I'm afraid my voice is more of a joyful noise than a sweet spirit, but it was from my heart nevertheless. Then I sang, In The Garden to Dad, while looking at Harrel's photo on the back of the bulletin, waiving good by to us left on this earth & his last statement being to remind everyone of his favorite scripture, John 3:16 .... Inviting all to accept Jesus as their Lord & Savior for the assurance of an eternity in Heaven! Amen!

The scripture reading, the Psalms & Apostles Creed & the Lords Prayer, reading it all, each time, gives me spiritual chills. How I wish we could have brought Mom there, but we just felt the trip would be impossible for her.

We have decided to make a donation to the Hospice that cared for Harrel, in lieu of flowers as you requested. Hospice was wonderful with Dad, they are a great organization. I have been in contact with a kind woman from your church via email, Vivian Matthews, & she is going to provide me with the address for Hospice.

Please know that we love you all, you will remain in our prayers & I'm sure we will be in touch soon. I am writing this on behalf of our whole family, Mom, Patti & Steve & family, Charles & our family, with continued love & affection.

A touching letter from Mike and Neva's daughter.

Harrel and Joan's family, taken at Harrel's granddaughter Tammy's wedding.

A Christmas card from the Shea Family of Fairmont Homes.

Chapter 11

Harrel and Darrel are indeed always thankful, but life has not always been a bowl of cherries in the mobile-home business. The Cohrons were—and are—incredibly successful, there is no doubt about that, and the business continues to thrive, but there were many bumps in the road along the way.

Some folks in town had it stuck in their heads that trailer parks were not welcome additions to the community. The Cohrons faced opposition many times over the years when they wanted to expand their business by adding more parks.

The local newspaper, the *Franklin Township Informer*, had a front-page headline on the August 14, 1986 edition that read: "Do we need another trailer park?"

In that same paper, on page three, the letters to the editor section included this letter from a local resident and business-man who obviously felt that the town did not need another trailer park.

Hello Everyone,

GOOD NEWS! We have come a long way toward **preventing** the re-zoning of 56+ acres of Franklin Township land to a trailer park. (Last week, we were given the impression that we couldn't do it—never say never.)

We have hired an attorney who is very familiar with the zoning system of zoning requests and petitions and site plans and file dates and zoning boards and continuances and appeals, etc etc etc.

The Franklin Township Zoning fund has been established. Several residents have already donated their first $100 to support the fund (which supports the legal costs). The Franklin Township Civic League has pitched in another $300—THANK YOU Civic League! Joan Asay is the treasurer. Her address is 6521 Churchman, 46237. We need YOUR financial investment—our bill could be in thousands of dollars.

Kathy Wilson is organizing the volunteer help that has been supplied thus far, passing out notices, arranging for transportation to the zoning hearing at 1:00 pm today, etc.

You've read the concerns of fellow township residents: the schoolchildren from the area would not be fully supported by the property taxes raised, the visual impact would affect property values, Churchman Avenue is inadequate for the traffic produced, and as always, we already have a water drainage problem.

We still have a lot to do. At this printing,
the particular zoning has been postponed.
Watch the *Informer* for the new date.

Have a good day,
Randy Faunce
Civic League NW Quad Rep

Later in that same paper there was an advertisement for Dr.
Randall Faunce, optometrist. Supporters of the Cohrons probably made a wise crack or two about the doctor needing to get
his eyes checked when it came to stating that mobile-home
parks' "visual impact would affect property values." Anyone
who had seen a Cohron Mobile Home Park would have to
say that they were all immaculate, up to date and lovely. Most
people think a property with a lake and a white-picket fence
would serve to increase property values.

This article appeared in 1986, nearly thirty years after the
Cohrons had started their business. For the Cohrons, it was
business as usual. They'd had to fight for the right to have their
trailer parks all throughout the years.

Back in 1980, when the *Lawrence Township Journal* cost
only twenty cents, the December 23 issue touted the front-page
headline "Zoning board approves new mobile home site." The
photograph that graced the page carried the caption, "Pro?
Con? The Lawrence City Building has standing room only at
Monday's hearing for rezoning land for a 103 unit mobile home
facility." The Cohrons certainly knew how to pack a room and
keep things interesting.

The article began: "The opinions of the crowd of 180 persons attending last week's zoning board meeting were quite evenly divided when the board considered a zoning variance request on an 81.02 acre plot between 46th and 52nd Street on Mitthoeffer."

The issue had been on the table the month before then, at the November meeting, but the vote had been split that night. The tiebreaker vote could not happen because a board member was absent. So, the debate happened again at the meeting right before Christmas—and with a full house. The property was actually owned by the Ellenbergers at the time, but it was common knowledge that the Cohrons wanted to purchase it.

One concern from the opposition was the proposed construction of a pond on the property to retain water and prevent flooding. A group of homeowners south of the site formed a group called the Outside Neighborhood Association, and they gathered 316 signatures—including seven from local realtors—to support the claim that drainage problems and traffic hassles would create a drop in their property values.

The group in favor of the zoning for the mobile-home park showed a filmstrip detailing the cost and convenience of mobile-home living that featured Rep. David Evans and Senator Richard Lugar. They both expressed their approval. Eighty homeowners from the Cohron-owned Greenbriar mobile-home park were present as well to show their support for the petition.

The group opposed to the petition that would allow the land to be rezoned for a mobile-home park continued their protest even after the board voted to approve the request. The Outside Neighborhood Association stated that they would appeal to a different commissioning board. The residents of Greenbriar stated that they would show up at that hearing as well to voice their support.

In the same spirit that the Cohrons have always displayed— sticking up for what you believe in without being overbearing about it—one mobile-home resident made a comment on the large crowd that had attended the meeting: "At least the people of Lawrence care."

It was indeed a caring community, and Harrel and Darrel Cohron have always been proud to be a part of Lawrence.

In any business, you win some and you lose some. Sometimes, zoning did not go the Cohrons' way, or plans for a property fell through. That was life. And they knew that life could not get mired in petty arguments.

———

The Cohrons have heard it all when it comes to mobile homes, and they want to dispel all the myths once and for all. There are so many stories about "trailer trash" that they long to put to rest. Any naysayers, they believe, should come out and visit one of their Cohron manufactured-home parks.

Many people think that mobile homes are built poorly with cheap materials. That is untrue. There are various levels of quality when it comes to materials; some cost less than others, just like it is with the building of any other home. If you get a framed stick-built house, the cost depends entirely upon what materials are used, and it varies tremendously from house to house.

When you are in a mobile home, you do not feel like you are in a trailer at all—though never everyone believes this. There is a myth that mobile homes are magnets for bad weather and cannot withstand strong storms. However, that is not true. Mobile homes are anchored and tied down in such a strong and thorough way that you're just as safe in one as you are in any type of home with no basement.

People are often led to believe that a mobile home is not a good investment. Nothing could be farther than the truth. A mobile home is like any other home: It does not depreciate, as many folks like to claim. As with all houses, a lot of factors and variables enter into the market value, such as the quality of the neighborhood, the standard maintenance and upkeep of the property, and, of course, location, location, location. In general, mobile homes cost less than a stand stick-built home, and in general, both increase in value over time. Resale value for mobile homes is the same as any other houses, too—if you have taken care of your home, when you sell it, you turn a profit.

Even in the turbulent economic times of recent years, mobile homes have kept their value, unlike "regular" neighborhoods and their constructions industries, who all took a hit when the economy tanked.

An article on Forbes.com in November 2008, said that American homebuilders had "dug themselves into a hole" by creating and then falling victim to the US housing bubble. It also predicted that when people are able to buy homes again, the same homebuilders will reap the profit—and that the *first* to profit will be the "humble" salespeople of the manufactured housing industry.

The Forbes article noted the appeal of mobile homes, saying that they have come a long way since the old-fashioned double wides. It also discussed how the federal government now includes manufactured homes in its tax-saving lending programs, which ups the appeal of mobile homes in general.

And *Forbes* isn't the only big name taking notice of the manufactured-home industry. Warren Buffet, the king of all American investors, has his hand in the mobile-home world as well. Buffet's company, Berkshire Hathaway, acquired mobile-home manufacturer Clayton Homes in 2003 for $1.7 billion. Clayton Homes is one of the top dogs in the industry, laying claim to about one-third of the market. Buffet's company also owns the two largest lenders in the mobile-home industry.

It's not surprising that Buffet, who is known for buying into any industry that shows a promising return on investment, has dipped his foot into the manufactured-homes pool, According to the Manufactured Home Institute, which keeps track of stats on sales and other related issues, manufactured-home sales accounted for about ten percent of the whole housing market in America in 2006. Due to the downturn in the market and the affordability of mobile homes, the institute predicts that the piece of the pie belonging to manufactured home sales will be near fifteen percent and continue to grow in the coming years.

One possible factor in this boom is the Housing and Recovery Act, an incentive passed by the Obama administration that makes it easier for folks to buy homes, including mobile homes. The new rules allow a loan of up $70,000 from the Federal Housing Administration for the purchase of a manufactured home. To qualify for such a loan, the buyer has to have a three-percent down payment and prove that he or she has the income to repay the loan. The caveat is that the loan is just for the mobile home, not for the land underneath it; however, that is true of most loans one could get to purchase a mobile home. Most mobile-home parks, including the Cohrons', collect rent on the land upon which each home sits.

Other incentives for people to buy manufactured homes include their affordability and amenities. Today's mobile homes feel like *homes*, not like a temporary trailer on camping lot, for example. And for what a buyer gets, the price couldn't be better. According to the aforementioned Forbes.com article, in 2007, manufactured homes went for about $40 a square foot. Stick-built homes cost more than twice that.

The prices of manufactured homes, the quality and the availability of financing make these homes attractive to many buyers. Cohrons only works with the top manufacturers and advise their clients that spending a little more upfront is worth the cost of preventing hassles down the road. The old adage "you get what you pay for" rings true in this case.

All homes the Cohron family sells are high quality, with top amenities. Their buyers get a lot of home for not a lot of money. The spring 2008 new-home price list is as follows; note that three of the top seven are from Warren Buffet's Berkshire Hathaway's Clayton Homes:

	Manufacturer	Size	Price
1	Norris	32 x 52	$89,995
2	Schult	28 x 55	$77,995
3	Clayton	28 x 72	$83,995
4	Clayton	32 x 64	$89,995
5	Clayton	32 x 64	$84,995
6	Fleetwood	28 x 60	$74,995
7	Dutch	32 x 76	$99,985

Where else can you get a brand-new, 2,400-square-foot home for under $100,000? Many people would not even think to look at a mobile home, but given these prices, the Cohrons wonder how anyone can pass up such a deal.

As Harrel states, "The names are varied: Trailer parks. Mobile-home parks. Manufactured-home communities. Land-lease communities. We say, call it home sweet home. Mobile-home parks are only as good as the people that live in them. Over the years we have met and had the pleasure to serve some of the most wonderful people in the world—our residents, our friends."

With an outlook like that, it's no surprise that the Cohrons claim that they enjoyed going to work every day and everything they did. To them, there were no career highs, no favorite deals. Though their careers spanned several decades, they claim now that everything they did could be called a highlight, because they just loved what they did so very much.

Chapter 12

Attitude is everything both at work and in life, though business smarts has to come into play as well. Harrel and Darrel have always been sharp, and they have made a lot of friends in the business world because of their win-win philosophy. They've never been greedy; they are in it to make a profit, but they have no problem sharing the wealth.

For example, in the early days of the 1980s, the Cohrons had a participation agreement with a financing company called Morris Plan. When the Cohrons sold a home, they would refer the purchaser to Morris Plan for financing. Morris Plan, in turn, would retain some of the proceeds of the deal and give the Cohrons due bills. When payments were made through a certain date, the Cohrons would take the due bills to Morris Plan and cash them in.

Harrel and Darrel believe that financing today would be better off if lenders used this form of agreement. They always liked to keep their financing options open. At Morris Plan, they worked with Mr. Goldsmith, who was the secretary-treasurer and John Shane, the manager. These relationships often led to more opportunities for both companies. For example,

Morris Plan had another client, a mobile-home dealer who floor planned thirty used homes but then quit paying for them. Mr. Goldsmith asked the Cohrons if they could take on those thirty homes and sell them for Morris Plan. Of course, Harrel and Darrel did it, further solidifying their good relationship with the financing company.

Another lending partner the Cohrons worked with was Indiana National Bank. John Steele was their man there, their go-to guy. Merle Stamps was their buyer. Merle was from Kentucky, and John would jokingly accuse the Cohrons of bribing Merle to buy their deals. According to Harrel and Darrel, John Steele was a great guy, and they enjoyed doing business with him.

Indiana National Bank was buying a lot of the Cohrons' paper, with Darrel and Harrel signing recourse on all of it. After a while, Indiana National Bank started to get a little aggressive. They began buying paper all over, and they got burned on some of it. So, they decided to quit financing mobile homes all together. The Cohrons thought that was too bad but understood how and why it happened.

"With Indiana National Bank," says Harrel, "we had eleven million dollars in recourse paper and all of it performed well enough. When you help the customer build equity by reasonable profits and shorter-term financing, it's a mutually beneficial relationship. We believe in that in all of our business dealings. Well, Indiana National Bank began financing mobile homes all over the place and got themselves in a pickle with some of them, and they ended up just cutting everybody off. But, for quite a while, we did have a good thing with them."

And that was the nature of business. Associates came and went; the Cohrons enjoyed good business deals and were sad, at times, to see them come to an end. Still, they did not let such disappointments get them down, and continued to look for new opportunities wherever they could.

Somewhere in their long history, a man from Foremost Insurance came calling. He set the Cohrons up to start selling homeowner policies on the homes they sold and introduced them to a man from American Fletcher National Bank. Their contact at AFNB was a man by the name of Sky Blue. Harrel and Darrel both remember thinking that was a funny name.

The next lender that the Cohrons hooked up with was Merchants Bank, where they worked with John Stainbrook and Ken Schilling. The two had been courting Darrel and Harrel's successful business for some time; in 1977, when the twins felt that the time was right, they finally agreed to work with them. Merchants Bank had a pay-as-you-go incentive program with limited recourse on certain deals. The Cohron brothers built up that book of loans into a considerable sum of money.

Here, again, the Cohrons enjoyed a great working relationship that lasted until Merchants Bank was bought out by National City Bank, which pulled back on mobile loans before too long. Dave Day was the buyer there, and Harrel and Darrel enjoyed working with him for a short time. "He was a great guy. He had a lot of lingo from the old days and we got along real well," Harrel recalls.

He also remembers how his excellent business relationships came in to help him and Darrel out in a pinch. "One time," he explains, "the bank was going through some tough times and we thought they were going to pull back on some of the loans. One of our manufacturers, the owner of Fairmont Homes, Jim Shea, put in a million dollars into a CD to keep our financing going. This was in the early eighties, I think."

That is exemplary of the trusting, helpful relationships that Harrel and Darrel cultivated.

The '80s were a tough decade when it came to money and financing; interest rates were very high, at eighteen to twenty percent. Harrel recalls, "Merchants Bank came out with a variable-rate program that did help our customers over time because the rates kept going down."

When National City bought out Merchants Bank, the Cohrons started their own finance company with some other backers and called it MHAC. Sure enough, though, National City cut them off on financing again. "They said it was due to too much exposure or something like that," Harrel recalls, "even though our portfolio was doing fine."

Still, the Cohrons continued to work well with the financers, giving them a lot of business over the years. This loyalty was recognized in a letter from Merchants Bank, which was immortalized on a handsome plaque and given to Harrel:

Dear Harrel:

As the '70s draw to an end, I would like to express my appreciation to you for the excellent business, cooperation and support that we have received from you. It has been a pleasure working with you and the other fine members of your staff throughout the years.

In looking to the '80s, we at Merchants look forward to continuing our fine business association with one of the city's finest dealers. We consider you a friend and truly respect the customer relationship that has developed between us over the years.

Again, many thanks for the excellent business you have sent to Merchants. My best wishes to you for continued success.

Sincerely,
John Stainbrook
Assistant Vice President

The next in the Cohrons' long line of financing partners over the years was Greentree and Security Pacific, which soon turned in to Conseco and Greenpoint. This company was fighting for market share. Harrel says, "With hindsight being twenty-twenty, I can see that their actions really sent our industry into a tailspin. They were financing homes with only five percent or less for down payments and giving thirty-year loans at subprime rates to subprime borrowers. I know it sounds familiar, huh? Our country is in the shape it is in because of these kinds of lenders and lending practices."

When Conseco eventually went bankrupt, Greenpoint ended up selling their portfolio to the Greentree people, who bought Conseco's loans out of bankruptcy. It sounds messy, but the Cohron family was always one step ahead of the game. By that point, they had their own financing sector under sons Bobby and Brad. This area has become a staple of the business' income.

The next finance company the Cohrons worked with was Fifth Third Bank, which unfortunately pulled back as well once the current economic crisis hit. The Cohrons now use MHAC and Clayton Homes and 21st Mortgage, a Berkshire Hathaway subsidiary.

Harrel and Darrel maintain that financing is not really all that hard of a concept to master. "You have to help a customer build equity, they need a down payment, you have to be selling something of value, and they need a job to pay for it."

Harrel and Darrel always give credit where credit is due and acknowledge the bumps in the road along the way as well. "We have had a lot of good relationships with our financing partners over the years," notes Harrel. "Other than that hiccup with Conseco, it has all been win-win."

Most of their dealings with mobile-home manufacturers have been win-win as well. In the early 1980s, Fairmont wanted the Cohrons to have an exclusive arrangement with them. Harrel and Darrel did not like that idea. They wanted to be able to use more than one manufacturer; they always wanted to have some options.

In the mid-1980s, Glen Hinton from Fleetwood Homes in Tennessee made a good presentation about their homes and won Harrel and Darrel over. They liked him and they liked the homes. So, they took Fleetwood homes into their inventory.

At that time, the twins recall, they were a little worried about the service on homes from another company, called Fairmont. The rep from Fairmont, Brian Shea, came for a visit and saw that the Cohron business now included Fleetwood homes, too. This was while they were still building out Briarwood Park.

Harrel explains, "Brian reported back to his father, Jim Shea, Sr., that we had Fleetwoods on our sales lot and in our parks. In the next week or two, we got a call from Joe Kimmel, our salesman at Fairmont, informing us that they were cutting us off. We were surprised. We would have kept doing business with them because we still had plenty of lots left to fill."

The next day, Harrel and Darrel sent Joe a dozen roses to thank him for all that he had done for them prior to this severance. The Cohrons still think that the Sheas are great people.

"We had a lot of fun," Darrel states. "We all made money doing business with them."

After losing the Fairmont Homes line, Harrel and Darrel went to another company, Holly Park, and took on their line of homes. They worked with salesman Joe Callahan. Not too long after that, the Cohrons' competitor, Young's Homes—which was only a half mile down the road—decided to sell Fairmont Homes. Harrel and Darrel are quick to point out that having a competitor so close by was not really a bad thing; there was no animosity between the two businesses. They all believed in the notion that a little healthy competition made everyone more successful.

Darrel says, "We've had a nice relationship with the Youngs over the years so none of this caused any hard feelings. They were also from Kentucky and we all got along pretty well."

Still, in order to remain competitive, Harrel and Darrel decided to start selling houses from Schult Homes as well. They developed a good bond with the folks at Schult—including Fred Todd and Larry Tompkins, who helped the Cohrons fill the lots at Quail Creek Park and Briar Creek. They wanted to offer their customers the best and most choices that they could—a philosophy that still drives the company today.

Chapter 13

"Hey, come and go with me." Darrel used that command over the years whenever he wanted to talk to Bobby about something. They worked together, but Darrel was always out in the parks or in the back with the guys. Bobby gravitated toward the office.

Some days, he'd get a call from Darrel, who said, "Come go with me. Let's go for a ride. I'll pick you up in the truck in five minutes."

Then, Darrel would pick him up, and they would ride through the parks and talk face to face, easily and conversationally, not confrontationally. Whenever he needed to talk something out, that was his way.

Bobby finds that the same method works well now with Matt, although they're both in the office together. It's just easier sometimes to clear their heads and to talk when they're away from the office.

While writing this book, Darrel called me up and said, "Come go with me." He wanted to take me on a ride through the parks to talk about their history and his history with brother Harrel.

"We were always partners, always," he began. "There was

never anything on paper. There really was never the question of who worked harder. Neither Harrel nor I ever counted hours or kept track of each other's time. We have run the business like farmers. We never held any grudges and we never stayed mad at each other.

"We know that life is a series of ups and downs. Some days are tough and some days are great. We had a common goal to do the best we could in this mobile-home business. I think I can say that our older brother, Paul, helped me the most with my work ethic. He was always a great example. But my whole family has been good to me. Paul and his wife, Mary, helped raise me and Harrel after our mom died. Sarah Dean and her husband, Walter, did too, of course. Walter was a great hunter and fisherman. Harrel and I certainly loved to do those things with him, too. They were awfully good to us.

"Harrel and I were the youngest. Paul was the oldest, then Dean. Getty, our next brother, went to Alaska to work on the electric lines there. Our other brother, Leonard, worked here with us. He was the park manager at Greenbriar for twenty-five years. He and his wife, Laurine—I always thought the world of them. We have a sister, Louise, and her husband is Jack. She is in Georgia so we don't get to spend much time with them. Then, of course, there was me and my twin. And we have known nothing else but spending time together.

"From the day we were born, we were looking out for each other and looking to one up each other. We were inseparable growing up. We went to school together in the one-room Little Muddy school. Then, we went to high school together up here. We both worked at Indiana Bell. We were drafted into the

Army at the same time, of course. We got on the ship; I think Dean had a hand in making sure we were in the same unit together. I know the story of our buying our Crown Victorias is already mentioned in here somewhere. The leftover money that we used to buy the first mobile homes and that little one acre is a story that I know is in here, too. That was how we got started—a little bit of cash and a little plot of land right here on Pendleton Pike.

"We didn't know then that we were launching something that would turn into a generational family business. We just were hard workers, wanting to make good money and do good for our customers.

"So much has happened over the years but my brother and I were always in it together. Vacations were the only time we spent apart. People talk about our scuffles, and they tell the truth. We had our run ins. If you spend that much time with your twin brother, it only makes sense that you have to air your disagreements. We operated under the same ground rules, though: Get mad. Throw something. Get over it and no hard feelings. Maybe to some, it looks like me and Harrel have quick tempers. Harrel gets reminded from time to time that he once slammed a door and the glass shattered. Not only did the glass break and go everywhere, but it went all over a customer. But with us, people know that we don't hold back. They know they are going to get the truth from us. We don't hold nothing back and that is just the way we are.

"You know Leroy, who came to work for us and stayed with us for over forty years. Leroy was like my brother, too. We didn't have the same kind of arguments, though. Harrel and I just had to vent, plain and simple. We got into some physical altercations, as they say. We each were just trying to make a point. And, we would go out back or behind closed doors to do so. If my shirt happened to get torn in the process, well, I'd just go home and change and come right on back to work. My wife never said a thing. Same with Harrel. He would laugh and say that the buttons were not sewn very well. He could run home and get a new shirt and we would go about our day. No hard feelings.

"That is part of the secret of our success. We don't keep anything bottled up. That doesn't do anybody any good. Speak your mind and move on. We have been successful in business because we trust our guts and we trust each other.

"When we started, that first year was all about selling used homes. We would buy and fix up and sell. We always paid as we went and did not have any debt. That gave us stability in the beginning. Then, when we started selling new homes and having models, things really expanded. Working with Les Bell, we paid as we sold the mobile homes. He treated us fairly and we developed a great business relationship and a great friendship. That is how we operate. We don't separate business from pleasure and we don't separate business relationships from friendships. Some of our best friends through the years have been the guys we have done business with. It only makes sense.

"The Donabell relationship was something special for us. Les Bell had been an accountant at Richardson Rubber. Don Rafferty was a farmer. They joined together and started Donabell. They opened an account with us and let us pay for our homes when they sold. This was what got us going in the new mobile-home business. It has always been one step at a time, and one thing leads to another and one relationship leads to another.

"The man who sold us our retail insurance, Earl Porter, introduced us to Fred Becher, who became our accountant. Then, eventually, Fred went off and started his own mobile-home business, which honestly did upset us a little. But, he ran into some rough times with that and it was our mutual friend, Karl Theyssen, who helped us to get Fred to do our books again. Fred and his wife, Rose, are two of the nicest people we know. We did a lot of social and family events with Karl and Fred and their families.

"Everyone we had contact with through the business—all of our subcontractors, our employees, certainly, our professional resources—we always treated everyone fairly. We did have mobile-home sales that went great guns in the early years, but we figured out that we had to be more than just a sales operation if we were going to make a go of this for the long term. The idea of having our own mobile-home parks made sense. And, it made dollars and cents.

"The parks and the sales feed each other. We knew we needed them both. We made the decision that in order to develop the parks, we would have to take on some debt, but we determined that no more than fifty percent of the cost of the park would be financed. This strategy meant we had less borrowed capital to repay, and so we were able to charge our residents lower rent. If we had been leveraged to hell, we would have had a heck of a monthly debt agreement to repay, so then we would have had to raise the rent in our parks. And, we're not like some of the other places that raised their rents all the time. We have low rent and it works for us.

"We give our business a personal touch. That really is all we know how to do—just be ourselves. I also firmly believe that a person has to love his business, whatever that business might be. If you are not in love with it, you are not going to make it. That is a piece of business advice that not everyone takes seriously, and I mean it. There is no replacement for hard work, but when you love what you do, it is so much easier to put in the hours and all the time and energy needed to make the business a success.

"Another piece of business is easy to say, but hard for some folks to adopt: You have to have a positive outlook. It makes all the difference in the world. Some people walk around thinking the world is out to get them. I don't. I have had maybe four or five bad days in my whole life. I know it was a bad day when my dad died, even though I was too young to remember anything about it. It was a bad day when my mom died, and I do remember that day. Leaving Kentucky was hard for me. It was home, and I was not sure what anything else would be like. Leaving our wives, Shirley and Joan, to go into the Army, that was a bad day. And, finding out that my brother, Harrel, is sick, now that was a bad day.

"But when you think of all the days I have lived so far in my life, more than twenty thousand, probably, to have had just few bad days shows that I have a good life. I have a real good life. I think we have shown our kids how to enjoy life, too. And how to run a business successfully, too.

"Sometimes, making business decisions with my brother would drive me nuts, no doubt about it. He would belabor a point every now and then, and it would drive me crazy. 'Just make a decision!' I would yell at him. I'd say to him that if he looked that hard at his wife, he never would have married her. He has got to be given a nudge sometimes. He has a good woman and so do I. They have put up with a lot over all these years. We worked long hours and they raised the kids. All of the kids have turned out great. They, in turn, have happy marriages and great kids, too. We have taught them to be genuine and honest. We are proud of all of our grandkids.

"My son, Bobby, and his wife live right next door to me. It is unique, I suppose, in this world, that we live that close and get along so well, but we do. He stops over every morning for coffee with his mom and me. At this age, he does not have to do anything to please me or his mother. He does it because he wants to.

"We have always taken it as a compliment when our residents have come into the office to pay their rent in person. They just want to say 'hello.' Sure, they want to save themselves the cost of a postage stamp, but we know our people. We like our people. And I have to say that I think they like us. They bring in great stuff for us, so that sure seems like it to me. Fried green tomatoes. Cakes. Cookies. Pies. Our residents are the best.

"Those signs in the parks that say 'we love our people' are not bullshit. We mean it."

Chapter 14

Bobby Cohron echoes what his dad has said. "If you look up the phrase 'people person' in the dictionary, you'll see my dad and his twin, Harrel. They are different in a lot of ways but share a lot of the same qualities, too. They are like a check-and-balance system for each other. That is why they work together so well and that is why their business has flourished."

Bobby states that his uncle Harrel is like a second father to him. He also does admit that he enjoys stopping by his folks' house each morning for a cup of coffee. "Sure, they bicker some, but their banter is actually a lot of fun," he reports. "My folks have a nice house now. I do, too. But they never forget where they started. Their first home was an eight-foot-by-thirty-five-foot mobile home. They still have a photo of it, and I had it blown it up for them. It is family-room wall art now."

To Bobby, his dad has always been a lot of fun. "He's one of those 'I can do anything' kind of guys. I remember when we were building Parkwood, he was out on a bulldozer. He was trying to move some dirt around for one reason or another and he probably did just fine doing that. But, Mr. I Can Do Anything didn't know how to turn off the damn bulldozer. He could have stayed out on that thing forever."

Bobby knows that he inherited his love of hunting from his dad and says that while they now usually go hunting where it's allowed, their days of hunting within the city limits were a lot of fun. "Except, of course, when we were busted or left out there," Bobby notes. "Then, my dad would make a smartass remark like, 'Don't worry, they can't eat you.'"

As most of the Cohrons' children report, Bobby's childhood memories are nothing but great. "My dad loved to go to car auctions," he recalls. "I loved going with him, too. We all had a lot of family fun in our everyday lives. It wasn't just all about the great vacations. I remember one time when Sheila wanted a dog, and not just any dog. She wanted a St. Bernard. So, when my mom was off at some Tupperware party or something, my dad went out and bought Sheila a St. Bernard."

Bobby admits that it might sound like the Cohron children were spoiled, but he insists that they were not really pampered at all. "We all had to work, and we were instilled with the value of work and the value of money. On my sixteenth birthday, of course, I wanted my own set of wheels. I had my eye on a pickup truck. We told Mom that we were just going to go look at it. She said not to buy it. We repeated that we were just going to look. Well, we bought it."

When Bobby and his dad got home, Darrel looked at his wife and said, "I had to."

"So, yeah," Bobby admits, "in a way we were spoiled—but not really spoiled rotten because we had good values instilled in us. And, we learned responsibility. I had to work and I had to earn money for that truck. It was not handed to me with a big bow on a silver platter."

Bobby attributes situations such as that one to his dad's propensity to be a spontaneous kind of shopper. "Not too long ago, he bought a couple of Vespa scooters for Matt and his wife," says Bobby. "It was a spur-of-the-moment kind of thing. He figured they would get a kick out of them, and they did. Matt got a red one and his wife got a pink one."

Surprises like that are not a new, thing, however, for the Cohron kids. "I remember how, when I was growing up, Dad would come home with things," Bobby remembers. "He was like a big kid in that way. He would buy things on a whim. Fun toys like go-carts, dirt bikes, four wheelers, golf carts, tractors, and sometimes dogs and horses. My dad was fun for me and Sheila when we were growing up, and he is a really fun grandpa for the grandkids and great grandkids."

Bobby has always enjoyed spending time with his dad, and going to work with Darrel and Harrel, he feels, was a natural course for his life to take. "I have always gone to both of them for guidance, and I still do. I grew up spending time here and working here, and I really love this business, too. It has been a lot of fun. I have no regrets. I liked working with my dad and now I get the pleasure to work here with my son, Matt. It is a pleasure. Working side by side with him is really special."

One of the best things about working at Cohron Homes, according to Bobby, is that it has always been stable; it provides great job security. "There's also the security of family here," he notes. "I'm just as comfortable in my office as I am in my living room in my house, and I think Matt feels the same way. He's been working here full time for almost five years now."

Even though it's been a while since Darrel called Bobby up

and asked him to go for a ride, Bobby will always think back fondly on those times. "I remember my dad using his truck as his office and the talks we had—and still have once in a while. I will always hear his voice saying to be at the back door in five minutes. Whenever I need to step away from the office, I do the same now with Matt. 'Hey, let's go for a ride' is code for 'hey, let's go have a chat.' We talk things out. We chew over ideas. If there is something on my mind or something on his, my car is the safe, private place where we can talk."

Bobby often thinks about how his dad and uncle built their business from scratch and looks proudly at what they achieved. "I don't mean the financial numbers," he says, "which are quite respectable, of course. I look at the hundreds of folks they feed at the Christmas barn party. I see all the happy kids and families who come to the strawberry festival. We give away over twelve hundred shortcakes in one day during the festival. I see the canned food drives and the charity stuff that they've done over the years. They realize that this community is what made us successful, and they have taught us that giving back is a way of life."

Everyone—even Harrel and Darrel themselves—joke about their famous "board meetings." Bobby concurs: "They had their spats, but you can ask anyone who has ever worked here and they will attest that there was never tension in the office. We all know of places where it's miserable to work and the tension is so thick that you can cut it with a knife. It was never like that here. They had their discussions and that was that. They didn't let things fester. They would blow up once in a while but like a quick storm, it passed and things were pleasant again. They could be ripping off each other's shirt buttons one minute and laughing until they were crying the next. And to hear them tell it, they would just say that the buttons must not have been sewn on so well and they just popped off."

These days, though Darrel is retired, he still finds time to help out around the office, and to Bobby, it's nice to see three generations of Cohrons working together under the same roof. "I love how my dad relates to my son at the office. Dad's retired now but still around and still willing to help. Matt knows that he can come to me or to his grandpa. He knows, like we all do, that we all are here for each other. My dad will pop in and drop a few zingers and share a little wisdom. He's always a lot of fun. He knows how to be successful and how not to flaunt it. He knows that a sense of humor goes a long way. I love it when he winks at Matt and quips, 'Do you think you will ever be as smart as me?'"

Darrel and Harrel have taught their children and grandchildren that having money does not automatically make someone a good person, that having money doesn't mean someone will pay their bills, and that people who don't have much money can be good, moral folks.

"One of the merits of Harrel and Darrel Cohron," says Bobby, "is that they treat everyone with the same level of respect. The guy who digs ditches is no better or no worse than the mayor. The construction workers and the bankers and the president of the United States are all worthy of the same respect and kindness."

Bobby asserts that these values can been seen in action at the barn parties and other functions that his dad and uncle Harrel host. "They attract people from all walks of life and these folks are laying down their guard and coming together to eat, drink and be merry. Harrel and Darrel can make people from all income levels and status classes get to know each other and see each other for the people that they are, not their bank accounts or titles or jobs or positions. They bring them all together and all you see is lots of laughing and talking and friendships happening. My dad always said, 'Go along and get along.' He practices what he preaches."

However, not everything is sunshine and rainbows for the Cohrons. They are not immune to the less-happy sides of life. "This is real life," Bobby notes, "and not everyone is pleased as punch all the time. And as you have learned, Harrel and my dad do not pussyfoot around. They are straight shooters and they give their honest opinions. There was a resident once who was mad at my dad over something, and he came in here to bitch about. He left just as mad. As he stormed out, he said, 'You are just as bad as that damn Darrel.' And you know what? I am proud of that. I am his son."

Chapter 15

Matt Cohron, the latest Cohron to join the family business, is proud to be Bob's son and Darrel's grandson. These days, he says that it was just a given that he would work at the family business. "I knew I would go to college, but I was not sure what I wanted to do for my career when I first went to school," he reports. "But I have no regrets about making this my career choice. I love working here."

Matt admits that he has learned a lot over the years from being around his dad and grandpa—things like timing, luck, perseverance and hard work, all of the ingredients for a successful business. "I believe in what my grandpa and Harrel have done here with this business," he says. "They've created good, clean, safe living for a lot of people. That's a very worthwhile thing. I also learned my grandpa's work ethic, so I come in early, I stay late and I tell the truth. It's so simple, but how many people do you know who actually adhere to that philosophy?"

According to Matt, things are a lot calmer around the Cohron Homes office than they were in the "good old days."

"My dad and my uncle Brad are not the same caliber of

characters as the twins," he says. "The twin factor is something that cannot be ignored and cannot be explained. I have heard the stories of Harrel and Darrel going at it. My dad and Brad do not argue in quite the same way. The stories of Harrel and Darrel's quarrels are why we wanted to capture some of the memories in a book.

"One day, they were fighting about something and they were back in the barn. They started picking up whatever they could find and hurling things at each other. There is a story about them throwing hammers at each other and Leroy out there, calmly ducking. I don't know if I am aware of any time that Brad and my dad threw things at each other."

Matt says that though Darrel and Harrel were reluctant to write a book about themselves, he understands the reason for doing so. "We wanted to try to capture their essence of goodness, their zest for live, their fun-loving natures and their down-home common sense that applies to life and business. They didn't want to seem like they were bragging. But when they warmed up to the idea, Grandpa Darrel suggested it be written as a horror story. I thought, *Why not a coloring book?* That's what's so fun about being a part of the family and the business—there's always joking, laughter and camaraderie. Those have been mainstays for the twins."

Matt seems himself as part of a new Cohron regime and is proud to carry on the family traditions. He adds, "I know that our business will continue for generations to come."

Chapter 16

Many voices from the "old guard" at Cohron Homes wanted to share their stories about Harrel and Darrel. One friend, Karl Theyssen, became a friend by doing work for Cohron Homes in the early years.

Karl had a business called AAA Heating; he did heating and air conditioning work for the Cohrons for thirty-five years. Karl recalls that in those days, the mobile homes had pot burners instead of gun burners, and he was one of the few who knew how to work on these heating systems. Karl remembers being in one trailer when the resident ran out of the house yelling, "It's gonna blow!" It didn't, though, and Karl was able to take care of the problem—and the agitated resident. After that, she went to the Cohrons and told them, "I found your new furnace man!"

The Cohrons gave Karl so much work, it just made sense to hire him as their furnace man. "Harrel and Darrel were sharper than hell," Karl says. "Nobody takes care of their customers like the Cohrons."

He also says, as has everyone else, that they fought like cats and dogs. Karl recalls a blowout at a Christmas party that involved a lot of back and forth between Harrel and Darrel, including the ripping up of a driver's license and the throwing of a fork. That last event cut Karl's lip, requiring a trip to the hospital.

Still, Karl enjoyed working—and playing—with the Cohrons. "We had a ball," he says. "One year, we rented a houseboat down on Kentucky Lake. In the process of getting down there, we had too much to drink. The guy at the boat place gave us the boat, but he would not give us the keys. So, the next day we got out on the water. We found a low spot and parked the boat. We took a sheet off of the mattress and tied it sort of like a net and scooped fish out of the lake. That was some great fishing. We had that big, fifty-foot houseboat and we decided to go frog hunting. We subsequently learned that you can't maneuver a boat that big down a pronged fork to go frog hunting. With Harrel and Darrel, things were always an adventure and always a lot of fun."

Karl also recalls driving to one memorable hunting trip in North Dakota with Darrel and five other guys. "We had a motor home and we would drive by day, and park and play cards by night. We were driving somewhere one day, in Iowa I think it was, and we ran out of beer. So, we went into a tavern to get some more. We learned that there were more pheasants there in that area than just about anywhere."

Darrel, being the great hunter and talker that he was, convinced the bar's owner to take them out pheasant hunting. "We were told where to go, and we showed up—a bunch of guys in a motor home—at some farmer's field. The farmer was out there, and Darrel took him a gift of whisky and asked to hunt his land."

In the end, the group got thirty pheasants that Karl recalls cleaning in the bathtub at a Holiday Inn. The next day, they went back again—and continued to do so for the next twelve years. "This farmer was not a drinker," Karl notes, "but he always let Darrel and whoever he brought hunt on his land. We even went to visit him last year on his eightieth birthday. That is how it goes with Darrel. He is always making friends and having fun."

According to Karl, Darrel and Harrel are just down-home boys, real down-to-Earth, outgoing, friendly gentlemen. "Darrel is not afraid to make a stranger a friend. That is how he enriches his own life and the lives of all those around him," says Karl. "He even invites himself to eat with people in restaurants. One time, he met a guy who had strip-mine ponds and went fishing a lot. So, of course, Darrel got invited to go fishing. In just an hour and a half, Darrel and the rest of us caught fifty-five big bluegills. I remember the owner saying, 'Now, if you don't come back and fish again, you will make me mad.'"

Darrel fired right back, "We'll be damn sure we don't make you mad!"

Karl always got a kick out of hanging out with Darrel and Harrel. He especially liked their running gag about being identical twins. "No matter what the offense," Karl recalls, "the one could always say, 'It wasn't me, it had to be my brother.'"

Despite their love of jokes, however, both of the Cohron

brothers would do anything for anyone. "I was honored to be their friend," says Karl. "Once, my office caught on fire and the Cohrons let me use the little building across the street from their office. That was their way—always willing to help."

They also were always willing to pull a gag. One time, during a group hunting trip, Darrel played a good one on their friend Ray Cummings. "We always bet on anything," says Karl. "Small potatoes kind of stuff, but always making a bet. Well, Ray had a new shotgun and unbeknownst to him, Darrel unloaded it, then told Ray that we had a five-dollar bet on the first rabbit. When Ray went to get a shot off, he pulled the trigger and there was nothing. Darrel, of course, laughed and held out his hand for his five-dollar payment."

There was always some kind of prank going on with the Cohrons. One morning, Karl woke up to find a bunch of real estate "for sale" signs in his yard.

They also liked to gamble. "We liked to roll the dice," Karl recalls. "One time I won and used the money to buy clothes for my kids."

Another time, while driving back from another hunting trip, they were playing poker in the back of the motor home and kept driving once they reached home because they wanted to keep playing. Another time, they picked up a hitchhiker. "We all wanted to drink and play and no one wanted to drive and miss out on the fun," reports Karl. "So, we stopped and picked up the hitchhiker to take care of that for us. He had so much fun, we couldn't get rid of him."

And that was what life was like with the Cohrons. "Once

you meet them, you want to be around them," says Karl, echoing what so many others have said about the twins as well. "They take care of their people—their friends, their family, their customers, their residents, everyone they come into contact with. We're all a little better for being a part of the Cohrons' lives and sharing their laughter."

Chapter 17

Everyone who knows the Cohron twins concurs that they like to take care of people. Many folks can tell stories about how Harrel and Darrel Cohron impacted their lives, and there are many individuals who influenced the lives of Harrel and Darrel as well. The Cohrons affect everyone they meet in one way or another, and the admiration goes both ways.

When the Cohrons see talent, they recognize it and act on it. This was the case with one resident, Carina, who used to be a property manager for a group of apartment buildings. In her Cohron home, she had an issue with her carport and instead of going through the Cohrons to get it taken care of, she did her own thing. In hindsight, she wishes she had gone to the company.

"They take care of residents' needs," she says. "They really do love their residents and want everyone to stay happy. It only makes sense, really."

Recently, the Cohrons hired Carina to manage one of the mobile-home parks. It was a perfect fit. She had the experience for that kind of job, she was willing to work for the Cohrons, and she speaks Spanish, so she can discuss housing issues with

Hispanic residents who are more comfortable conversing in their native language.

As Woody puts it, "That was the one of the best moves Harrel and Darrel ever made. Times are always changing, and you need to change with the times. Carina is a great gal and is great with the residents. Hiring her was real smart."

Darrel simply adds, "I had to hire her. She was the only one who stood up to me."

Although, that is not exactly true—Darrel's wife, Shirley, is pretty good at standing up to him, too. Darrel likes to joke with people who can dish it and take it. He hits if off with most everyone but especially enjoys bantering with those who can keep up with him.

At work, Harrel and Darrel welcomed everyone they met into their lives and everyone became a friend. Walter, the mailman, became more than the guy who brought letters and packages. Now, he is a friend. He no longer even has the Cohron business on his route, but he still stops by to chat.

"After seeing someone every day, you don't just drop them," Walter says. "I have been helped tremendously by my talks with Harrel over all these years. A few years back, I was going through a divorce and it was really difficult. Harrel helped me out."

In today's hectic world, too many business owners do not see people, just job titles. They don't make time to talk to the mailman or cultivate relationships, and so they miss out on great friendships. Harrel and Darrel always have time to talk.

Part of the strength of the Cohron family comes from the fact that they share the power. They help out all the other businesses in town with their referrals. From the guy who makes signs to the company that makes the annual calendars for the mobile home parks, the Cohrons like to give their business to companies they trust.

Every new resident of a Cohron Homes park gets a list of supply and repair companies that the Cohrons have dealt with for over twenty years. They have these "park approved" service companies because the Cohrons want their residents to get their problems taken care of properly. The list provides manufactured-housing supply companies, service supplies, home-repair companies, lawn-care services and utility companies. Being on the Cohron list must certainly be a boon to all the companies it includes. The Cohrons have always been about community support. They don't just talk about it; they do it.

While they were in business, Darrel and Harrel were famous in Indy for their antics, but they were also well known in the community for their generosity. They never made any kind of donations as attention-getting stunts. They gave because they felt compelled to give back to the town that had done so much for them.

The second mayor to take office in Lawrence while the Cohrons were in business was Bob Sterrett. He became mayor in 1984, when the population of the town was about 20,000. It is now over 40,000 strong, Bob has always admired the Cohron twins and can attest to their generous giving to the many needs of Lawrence over the years.

"When it comes to community involvement," Mayor Sterrett says, "Harrel and Darrel Cohron were knee deep in it. They gave generously and they have done so much anonymously. That is real giving. They give to give back, not to get attention or to give themselves a pat on the back."

Harrel and Darrel always gave to the larger causes, like the police and fire departments, but there were so many other donations they made just because they were good, warm, caring human beings. Mayor Sterrett recalls a time when there was a fire in one of the Cohrons' mobile homes. "It was just three days before Christmas," Bob notes, "and this guy lost his home and possessions. His spirit was slumping."

In response, the Cohron twins cleaned out an old mobile home in one of their parks and gave it to this guy to live in while he waited for his own house to be repaired. And, they did this anonymously. "I imagine a Christmastime good deed would have gotten them some good free press," says the mayor, "but they kept it quiet and just did it to help this man out, not to give themselves free publicity."

Mayor Sterrett calls the Cohron brothers true pillars of the community and says that he always knew he could count on them for anything that came up. "They were like secret angels or secret Santas or something. If I got wind of someone needing a little helping hand, Harrel and Darrel were always willing to help out. It could have been someone who was down on their luck and needed a car fixed. I could mention it to Harrel and Darrel and the money would appear."

Harrel and Darrel Cohron were, in reality, simple boys who grew up to be simple men with a bit of wealth. They always appreciated their roots as well as the good fortune they came to know. They gave to organizations and they always wanted to help any individuals in town who needed some assistance to get by. "The Cohrons were pranksters and loved a certain kind of attention, but they shunned publicity," says Mayor Sterrett. "They gave to give. The old philosophy that 'givers get' really mattered to them. They both were very generous with their time and their money."

Many communities have their "fortunate sons" who always get called up for charitable donations. Harrel and Darrel never tired of giving and never questioned it. They went above and beyond the call of duty. Not only did they give to anyone and everyone who came knocking, but they recruited others to give as well.

That spirit of generosity and compassion is what really sets the Cohrons apart from the rest of us," says the mayor. "They were like an unending well of giving and kindness. Harrel and Darrel rounded up the other business leaders in town to give money for city employees. They knew that the mayor's office did not have a budget for that kind of thing, but they thought that everyone deserved a nice Christmas luncheon. Of course, they did their big barn party every year, but because of them, city employees got to have a small recognition of appreciation as well. The guys who plow the streets and the other municipal employees were forever grateful, let me tell you."

The local schools will sing the Cohrons' praises, too. Besides the old covered wagon that Darrel donated to a local elementary school, the brothers have always been extremely generous with monetary donations. "Maybe those are the two words that best describe Harrel and Darrel," notes the mayor. "Extremely generous."

The Cohrons' barn party, of course, is legendary in Lawrence. On the Friday before Christmas, they clear out all the equipment from the big barn on the back of the sales lot. They lay out quite a spread—venison, ham, turkey and all the trimmings. They fill tubs with soft drinks and not-so-soft drinks. The entire community is welcome, including their park residents, the bankers they deal with and all the businesspeople in town. You name it, everyone stops by.

"It really is a party," says Mayor Sterrett. "It's been a tradition around here since the nineteen seventies."

Each June, the Cohrons host a strawberry festival and turn the sales lot into a gathering place for the whole community once again. This event is more of a family affair. They have strawberry shortcake and ice cream for literally thousands of people. They give it away for free, just to say "thank you" to their residents and the community folks who come out. The kids love it; there's face painting and balloons and every child gets a toy.

"It's sort of like Christmas in June," notes the mayor.

The Cohrons truly care about their residents, their mobile-home parks and the community of Lawrence. As Mayor

Sterrett says, "They are characters, for sure, but they are not law breakers and they want a safe place, a town free of crime for all of us. Back in the eighties, they learned that one of their residents was selling drugs from his home. They have zero tolerance for that kind of activity. They had this guy's trailer jacked up off its ties, and they marched over there and told him that he was gone, out of there. They said, in no uncertain terms, 'You are not living here. Where do you want us to move this trailer? Because you are not staying here.'"

Mayor Bob Sterrett has the utmost respect for the Cohron twins and claims that while everybody knows that Harrel and Darrel can get testy with each other, they are as gentle as lambs with everybody else. "And now, I look at their boys, who have taken over the business, and I see their dads in them," adds the mayor.

Harrel and Darrel have a sense of fun and, yes, a sense of mischief. They loved to play cards back in the day, and their dice games are legendary. "When they were younger men, I think they felt they were bulletproof. We all did, I guess," says Mayor Sterrett. "They've experienced tremendous success and they have not let it go to their heads—or their hearts."

However, the mayor does recall some times when he thought the Cohrons might have gone a little bit off their rockers. "I remember one year," he says, "when these nuts hired the chief of police to drive them to the Daytona 500."

In addition, back when Mr. Sterrett first took over as mayor of Lawrence, he got a call from the police chief. "Mr. Mayor," the chief said, "the brothers Cohron are out hunting again."

"The twins used to make any land their own hunting

ground," the mayor recalls. "They each ended up buying property to hunt on. You know what they say—you can take a boy
off the farm but you can't take the farm out of the boy. That is
really true."

It's also true that the Cohron brothers and their families
have made a lasting impact on the city of Lawrence. "You can't
take the Cohrons out of Lawrence," adds the mayor. "They are
forever a part of this town. And we are forever grateful for all
that they have done."

Chapter 18

Behind every good man is a good woman. Harrel has Joan and Darrel has Shirley. Behind every successful company is an organized and efficient secretary. Maybe the word "secretary" is becoming outdated, but every office needs someone who can take care of all the details, give customer service with a smile and compassion, and pass out the paychecks on Friday afternoon.

The Cohrons have had a few gals who could keep all the plates spinning and all the balls up in the air. For the past twenty years, Liz Riester has been the go-to gal to keep the place running smoothly. For the Cohrons and Liz, it is a mutual admiration society.

Liz started working at Cohron Homes in 1988. She was recommended by Karl Theyssen and then interviewed with Harrel. They discussed office work overall and her knowledge of computers. The Cohrons had just implemented a computer system.

After they talked, Harrel said he would call Liz back, and he did. Then, she went in again and talked to Bob Woodhouse, along with Harrel. He hired Liz the next day.

"I've been with them twenty years now and enjoy my job very much," Liz reports. "The Cohron family is really great to work for, and they're very considerate of their employees. I lost my father while working here and anytime that I needed off while he was in the hospital or afterwards was no problem. They never questioned anything, only asked what they could to do help me."

Liz also had a young son who played sports, and she never had to miss a game because of work. As long as she got her work done, Darrel and Harrel had no problem letting her go to watch her son play.

"I'd say that's pretty fair," says Liz. "Family is always first with the Cohrons."

Honesty is also huge with the Darrel and Harrel. "I remember when I was hired," Liz says. "Harrel told me two things: Don't lie to him and don't call him a liar. He said if I could do those things, then we would get along just fine. And we did."

Over the years, Liz witnessed just how good the Cohrons were to their customers. Darrel and Harrel truly wanted the people in their parks to be happy in their homes and with their experience with the company.

"We all received a copy of the book *Hug Your Customer* one year," Liz recalls. "It was a great story about a company that really made it big by going the extra mile for their customers. The Cohrons have always done that, too."

Liz also notes that if either Darrel or Harrel gives you his word, that's it. "You don't need it in writing. They stand behind what they say and that goes for everyone," she says. "If we go out on a limb and promise something to a customer, the Cohrons will stand behind that, too. I think we have a great crew that uses good common sense, and it works well all the way around."

With the third generation of Cohrons now running the business, Liz feels confident that this tradition of outstanding service will continue. "Matt Cohron is made of the same good stuff," she opines. "I really enjoy working with him and you can tell that he really enjoys the business."

As Liz and so many other of Cohron Homes' employees relate, working for Darrel and Harrel really is like being part of a great big family. "We kid around with each other, go through tough times together, and work hard together," Liz says. "But it's always enjoyable. I love them all."

Chapter 19

Harrel and Darrel Cohron are an American success story. Starting out as poor fellows from Kentucky who lost both their parents when they were very young, they learned to make a go of it on their own—and many people find that inspiring. Their positive outlook on life is contagious and they show that anyone can become a millionaire if he or she works hard enough. And throughout it all, they've had no complaints and no regrets. They are just proud of their family and their family business.

Brad Cohron says that even now, some people have wrong ideas about mobile homes and mobile-home parks. The old notion of trailer parks as dirty dumps with dogs on chains and "trailer trash" people refuses to fade away. And the Cohrons admit that such places do exist—but not in a Cohron neighborhood in Lawrence, Indiana.

"My dad and my uncle worked their whole lives to dispel the myths about mobile homes," Brad says. "They faced a lot of opposition to zoning in the early decades. People fought to keep something out that they honestly didn't know anything about. We still see that occasionally in our business. We've all seen people who are prejudiced against something that they really know nothing about."

Cohron mobile homes are quality built and have all the amenities of any other kind of home, and the Cohron Homes neighborhoods are built exactly the same. The Cohron communities are places where neighbors get to know each other and look out for each other. All of the Cohron mobile-home parks are clean, safe and well kept. The residents keep up their properties and the Cohrons maintain the roads and all the common areas. The are in good locations with good schools, so they attract good families. They even feature white-picket fences, lakes and playgrounds.

As Brad puts it, "We don't have to take every Tom, Dick or Harry. The Harry we don't want goes to one of the other parks and ends up paying higher lot rent for a place that is not as nice. We have standards for our homes, our parks and our residents. We carefully screen our customers and if they are not creditworthy or don't have jobs or don't give the indication that they're serious about being able make their monthly payments, we do not accept them.

Now that the Cohrons carry seventy-five percent of their financing, their ability to judge character is more crucial than ever. They carefully screen and evaluate all potential residents, to try to discern what kind of people they are before allowing them to move in. However, that doesn't mean that they aren't willing to give someone a chance.

"If a person has lousy credit, but I can tell by talking with him that he has a job and really wants this home and a fresh start, I will give him the loan. Our residents are great people. We respect their dedication to us and we want them to live in neighborhoods and homes that they can be proud of. We're proud of our homes. Our business wouldn't be what it is today if we didn't have the product and the integrity."

And that was why, Brad believes, it bothered Darrel and Harrel so much when, back in the early days of their business, they met so much opposition in the city of Lawrence. "It was sort of like a slap in the face," he says. "They had the support of all the residents who already lived in their parks. That's very telling. If my dad and Darrel were slumlords, no one would have vouched for them. We have a whole community that will vouch for us now. Thanks to the hard work of Harrel and Darrel Cohron, hundreds of people in Lawrence have beautiful, safe places to live. My dad and Darrel never veered from their passion and that loyalty has been returned a hundredfold over the years."

As the twins' sister, Dean, once said, "Harrel and Darrel could live to be two hundred years old and the mobile home business wouldn't ever get out of their blood."

In those early years, when some of the locals were fighting against the Cohrons' application for zoning for a mobile-home neighborhood, there was one woman who said, "If you let those Kentuckians put in a trailer park here, this whole end of town will be nothing but trailers."

Darrel summed it up perfectly when, with a wink and a nod, he declared, "And that's exactly what happened."

Chapter 20

The success of Harrel and Darrel Cohron comes from their being equal parts wise men and wise guys. They both embody the perfect combination of wit and heart and are very grateful for all the good fortune that has come their way. They have never taken their abundant blessings for granted.

There is a page from a devotional book that always meant a lot to both Harrel and Darrel. It is a brief commentary on the wealthy icon J.P. Morgan:

J.P. Morgan's Wealth and God's Mercy

When the multimillionaire J.P. Morgan died, his will consisted of about 10,000 words and contained 37 articles. But we are left in no doubt as to what Mr. Morgan considered to be the most important affair in his whole life. He made many transactions, some affecting large sums of money. Yet there was evidently one transaction of supreme importance in Mr. Morgan's mind. Here is what he said: "I commit my soul into the hands of my Savior, in full confidence that, having redeemed and washed it in his most precious blood, he will present it faultless before my heavenly Father, and I entreat my children to maintain and defend, at all hazard and at any cost of personal sacrifice, the blessed doctrine of the complete atonement for sin through the blood of Jesus Christ, once offered, and through that alone."

In the matter of his soul's eternal blessing, J.P. Morgan's vast wealth was powerless. He was as dependent upon mercy as was the dying thief at Calvary. He was dependent upon the mercy of God and the shed blood of Christ just as you too are dependent.

In Memoriam

Harrel Cohron passed away on December 30, 2008. He was under hospice care and was able to die at home with Darrel and his wife near his side. The *Indianapolis Star* published his obituary and a feature article by reporter John Tuohy, which opened with:

> Identical twins Harrel and Darrel Cohron grew up in Kentucky together, moved to Indianapolis together, and started a mobile home business together. So when Darrel spent the last few days of Harrel's life lying beside him in bed, comforting his brother while cancer sapped his strength, it surprised no one.
>
> "He was right there with him, sleeping in the same bed," said Brad Cohron, Harrel Cohron's son. "He knew how sick he was."

About a thousand people attended the memorial service for Harrel at Servants of Christ Lutheran Church in Lawrence, of which Harrel was a founding member. He was also a member of Masonic Lodge 726.

Harrel was awarded the Sagamore of the Wabash distinction, an award honoring the favorite sons and daughters of Indiana, for his significant contribution to life in the state. The award has been bestowed upon ordinary people who have shown outstanding service, such as volunteers, veterans or educators, and upon presidents, astronauts, entertainers and entrepreneurs. Harrel certainly qualifies as an extraordinary entrepreneur.

The article in the *Indianapolis Star* also stated what everyone already knew: that Harrel and Darrel's differences in personality made a perfect fit for the business. They had the classic Mr. Inside and Mr. Outside arrangement. Darrel said, "I liked to walk the grounds of the parks, and he liked it in the office, a born salesman."

Paul Ricketts, the mayor of Lawrence and a longtime friend of the family, commented that the Cohrons have been important in the civic life of the town for years. He called them "notable contributors" to many police and fire causes. He also mentioned that the Cohrons' mobile-home parks have been good for the city in two ways: They have given the city a solid tax base and provided affordable, clean and safe housing for many people.

At the time of his passing, countless people poured out their hearts and their stories about the joy and caring that Harrel displayed. Thousands of dollars were donated in his memory to the Servants of Christ Mission Endowment Fund at his church.

The Cohron family loved to hear the stories. They all have their own special memories of Harrel and it was a comfort to hear the love and respect that others share for their brother, father, husband and uncle.

The family also received many letters regarding Harrel and his impact on the lives of those who met him, including the following:

Dear Brad and Family,

I just wanted to share a very heartwarming story about your dad. In April of 1979, my mobile home burned down completely. My insurance company wanted me to stay at a motel for six weeks while I was waiting for my new mobile home. I called your dad and he put some furniture in an empty mobile home so that I could stay there. I was very grateful because I was raising my daughter without any support.

When I received a check from my insurance company (made out to me and the Cohrons), I signed the check and your dad signed the check, and then he gave the check back to me. He said, "You need this more than we do." And I can't tell you how grateful I was, for this helped my daughter and me in so many ways. I feel this selfless act may have saved my life.

Thank you for everything.
Emma Sue R.

At Harrel's funeral on January 5, 2009, Mayor Paul Ricketts read a proclamation in Harrel's honor. He spoke of Harrel's devotion to the community of Lawrence. Those in attendance were also asked to sing Harrel's favorite hymn "The Old Rugged Cross," which had also been sung at his mother's funeral. They also sung "A Mighty Fortress Is Our God" and "Amazing Grace."

Harrel's grandson, Travis, spoke eloquently at the service. He said, "My grandfather lived life completely and intensely. His life was a testament to hard work and a positive outlook. He had wisdom, which he shared with us. He told me: Touching ten different hot stoves is no different from touching the same one repeatedly. They all still burn."

Travis went on, "My grandfather was intelligent, charismatic and occasionally defiant, and certainly had his own brand of humor. One of the stories that comes to mind is when he claimed he could catch a seagull with his bare hands. And, of course, he did. Which of course prompted the seagull to defecate on his head. He was a character, but he was a deep thinker with a progressive mind. He felt deeply and he was always kind. We give our grandmother the credit for her kindness rubbing off on him."

In conclusion, Travis noted, "John F. Kennedy once said, 'Some men see things as they are and ask why. Some men see things as they could be and ask why not.' My grandfather was one who asked why not. Why not applied to two brothers born into poverty and overcoming all obstacles. They made their dreams into reality. They grew up without the love and warmth of two parents yet had families that never had to endure such hardship."

Brad's son, Jacob, got to spend a lot of time with his grandpa in the year before his death. They would drive around on errands or go down to the lake house, which gave them hours in the car to talk. The overriding themes of all their conversations, no matter what the topic was, were friendship and helping others.

Harrel always said that his favorite movie was *One Flew Over the Cuckoo's Nest* because the characters reminded him of his friends. To those who know the movie, that might not sound like a compliment, but to Harrel it was. Jake said, "He always said it's important to have friends you can depend on and to be a friend that others can depend on. He was a man full of life and always surrounded by friends."

At the viewing, on the night before Harrel's funeral, among the photos and memorabilia was a small stuffed alligator. According to son Bill, that was the actual gator from a fishing trip to Florida many years earlier.

The story goes that Harrel and his fishing buddy were in the boat, having a rousing conversation; Harrel had always enjoyed people who could dish it out as well as take it. In the middle of their banter, Harrel reached into the water and scooped out this little alligator and threw it, teeth first, at his fishing partner. How the critter died and got himself stuffed is still a mystery.

Harrel Cohron had a sense of humor that permeated everything he did, and he inspired those who loved him to shed tears not just of sadness but of laughter at his funeral. That is a real testament to his character—and to the character of the entire Cohron family.

Aside from being a real jokester, however, Harrel was also quite serious about his faith. He gave his time and his talents to his church and community; he did not just give financial contributions but lent his energy and ideas to help many people in many ways. In his casket at the viewing, there was a copy of Leonardo da Vinci's "The Last Supper," which had hung in Harrel's dining room at home for many years. As Harrel had always said, "If you want to get in this picture, you have to get yourself on the right side of the table."

Harrel always knew that he was blessed, and he lived a life of gratitude. He wanted to share his wealth, good fortune, good heart and love of life with others. Harrel loved his business and his hobbies of hunting and fishing, but more than anything he loved his family and his friends. He will be deeply missed. This book is dedicated to his memory.

Postscript of Random Thoughts

To prepare for this book, the Cohron family made audio recordings of Harrel and Darrel answering some questions. Now that Harrel is gone, it is poignant to have his voice on tape. Hearing the stories in his words brings them to life. The following is a transcript of some of his recordings.

I can see Old Muddy. It was just a little, brick building with the church, a little, one-room schoolhouse, all the grade levels in here together. Yep, we had to walk a mile to school.

Mike Michaels gave me my first job at fifty cents an hour. He hired me and didn't even tell me what he was gonna pay me. I was maybe fifteen years old that summer. I said I wanted a job; he said, "What can you do?" And I said, "Anything you want me to do." I cleaned the cooler out—there was a cooler that kept lunchmeat and other things. I cleaned it out and there were maggots in there. Keeping the bathrooms clean was part of my job.

After those first tasks were done, he asked me what I had done, and I told him. He said, "You can go ahead and eat lunch now. You can eat whatever you want from the cooler and drink all the pop you want. Don't eat the yellow bananas, though. You have to eat the brown ones. Write your hours down on a piece a paper."

At the end of the week, I had turned in eighty hours and he paid me forty bucks. I went home and told my sister I wasn't going to school no more.

He had maybe fifteen trailers and that little store. Mike and his wife, Neva, eventually moved to California, but they came back for our sixtieth birthday party. Mike was maybe only fifteen years older than I was, but that seemed like a lot more years when I was fifteen. Now, it's nothing.

He was quite a guy. A good salesman, but no detail, no detail at all. He had trailer sales there. Sales now is what I like best, more than any other part of the organization. I learned a lot from Mike. I have no regrets. I enjoyed every minute of it. I look back now and maybe I should have been a little easier. I'm the type of guy—when I want something done, I want it done. I get it done, I expect others to get it done. Maybe I have a hardnosed work ethic. I would say it is a good work ethic. My brother, Paul, taught me that. He's a farmer; he's a real hard worker. There is not any horsing around with him.

This guy taught me how to sell. He was super salesman. He could sell anything. I had to listen to him and I learned a lot. The sad thing was he had a real weakness for alcohol. I tried to help as much as I could but you know what they say, a person has got to help himself. He got pretty bad and let things go. They ended up moving to California. I think it was Riverside, California. His wife got a real good job out there, at a place that made airplane parts, I believe. Some defense-contract kind of place. She had a good job and had insurance and a good pension. She took care of things.

His wife, Neva, was a good Christian woman, a good Baptist girl. They had two little baby girls, beautiful girls. I used to babysit those girls. Changed their diapers. Now they are grown up and gorgeous. One is a beauty queen. But his wife, Mike's wife, was a real good woman. She was the glue that held that family together. She worked her job, and he sold pickles and drove taxi cabs.

In the early days of me working there for him, I used to go run errands for him and that would include buying him booze. I would go to the liquor store and buy a fifth of whiskey. I don't have my driver's license yet mind you and here I am driving his truck and going to the liquor store.

He would have me get him a pint or half a pint. One day I swore I went to the liquor store four times in one day for him. I said, "Why don't I just buy you a big gallon jug instead?" He said, "Only drunks do that." Or he'd say that he'd get too drunk if I bought it all at once. I said, "Hell, you are drunk by two o'clock anyway."

He was a character and a half. Mike was a real good man. He had it rough from the beginning. He was adopted. He was real young and he hawked the girly shows at the fairs and festivals and carnivals. He would do the big talking to get men to pay their nickels to go inside the tent and see the women. So Mike was always talking about girls. He came by it when he was young and naturally. That was his life. Working with him was always interesting. Every day he talked about girls.

He was real likable, real personable. People liked him. All

the folks that lived in his trailer park would come in to pay their rent at the grocery store there where I worked. You see, I came from Kentucky and I don't even know my way out the front door. Folks would come in from my school and ask for sanitary napkins. I didn't know what the hell they was asking for. So I went back and asked Mike what the heck that was. "That's Kotex, you dumb SOB."

He called me that more than once. His grocer store and trailer lot was on East Washington Street or Highway 40. A guy came in and asked, "Where's Highway 40?" I didn't know where Highway 40 is so I went back to ask the boss. He says to tell him to take a right and then at the stoplight, take a right and that's 40. So that is what I did. The next day Mike asked me if I directed that guy to Highway 40.

"Yeah, I told him what you told me." He pointed out the front glass window, directly across the street. The sign said Highway 40. Highway 40 and East Washington are the same road.

"Dumb shit."

No one can do it by themselves. I had help in my life. I had my twin brother and my family.

Computers are good or bad. Depends upon when you were born. Computers are wonderful things, you know, in some cases, but I don't need them.

If you don't have a good woman you ain't got nothing. If you ain't got a good woman, you ain't gonna make it.

My wife and I were both from big families. She was one of nine kids, my family had seven. We had a family reunion on her side and 300 people showed up. My religion helps some, too. I was Lutheran and my wife is from the Lutheran tradition, too. She never did try to force anything on me. A lot of people try to force their ways and views on you. She was never like that.

And when it comes to selling, I had a lot of intuition. You might not have good credit but you come in and want to buy a mobile home. We sit down and I would talk to you. If you have a job, a decent job, that is what matters. If you have a job and I can determine from our interview time that you would be able to pay, I will take you on. If you tell me you're a go-go girl, I won't, but if you tell me you're an office girl down the road at AT&T, I'm going to sell you a mobile home before you get out my office. I'll interview and I'll make the loan. It has worked very well for us.

At one point, we held 100 homes at one time. Those were gangbusters years.

I have a gift from God, I think, and part of it is teaching yourself how to deal with people. We all judge people. You'll make a judgment call on me. It can either be good or bad, but we all make those judgments. So many people think they have to lie to get anywhere and that is just not true. That's always a big no-no. The first question I ask is the important one: "Where do you work at?" That can tell me everything that I want to know. If you don't have a job, I don't think I will be able to sell you a mobile home.

Over the years I have had fifteen salesmen. One guy lasted

two days. Then, look at Woody. He lasted a lifetime. I couldn't run him off. He showed up every day. He minded me. He listened to me better than my wife or anyone else ever did. Every day we would have our coffee at 8:30 and be ready for work at nine. He has a beautiful wife, too.

Dean is one of the beautiful people, too. She was like a Mother Theresa in my life. We lived with her and she raised me. She moved here to Indy when we were still in Kentucky. We didn't have a telephone back then. She would send penny postcards. We would get a card saying, "I'll be home Friday night."

By the time she would get off work and make the long trip on those bad roads like they were back then, she did not get home until ten o'clock. She would always bring us something. It didn't make a difference really what it was—we were just always excited when Dean come home and excited to see what she brought us. Maybe it was a pair of blue jeans or a pair of overalls or little candy. Even if it was just nickel-and-dime stuff, she always thought of us. We would stay up till ten o'clock so we could see her and see what she had for us.

We then came up here to live with her. We lived with her and her husband all through high school. She is a great cook and she fed us.

(On raising kids.) You're doing them a disgrace not to have them learn how to take care of themselves. You're not going to be around forever, you know. My wife did a great job raising the kids. I brought the money home. She raised the kids.

(On helping friends.) One friend, oh, I think I helped him

out twenty different times. These were not loans with expectation of repayment. It was a gift.

(On business.) Some people would come into the lot and say, "You're higher than the guy down the street." I know I am. I have to charge more because I sell a better product. Think of merchandise sold by the pound. Take my mobile home and put it up on the scale. Mine will weigh 3,000 pounds more than the guy down the street and so it is going to cost $3,000 more. I would explain, and I would just show them. We have always believed and still do believe in educating our customers.

You have to be smart enough to know your product and your business, or you don't have any business being out here trying to sell someone something.

I can keep you dry, I can keep you warm, and I can set you in a nice, safe neighborhood—a place where you can get along with your neighbors. And that's up to me.

I won't loan money to anybody. I'll give it to you, but I won't loan it to you. Money deals that don't work out can hurt a good relationship. I gave John $3,900 for that antiques business deal that totally went south. I never did that again. I learned my lesson. I told my wife it was like paying four grand for a college education. I took it on the chin, but I learned.

Over the years, I gave money to different friends. They might have called it loans. I have maybe $50,000, maybe even close to $100,000 that I've lent to people over a fifty-year period. All small amounts. Just a little something to help people get by when they ran into a snag in their life. Biggest amount is maybe only four or five thousand. I tried to help them out of a rut. You know, but then they don't even speak to you afterward. They didn't pay it back, so they feel like that they can't face me. Shit, I don't give a damn.

(On the big, dead animal on the wall at the office.) People think the mighty hunting Cohron clan brought back their kill. It's from one of their trips, alright. Harrel wanted to buy it from a bar one night but the bartender or bar owner wanted seven, eight, nine hundred dollars for it. Hell, I ain't paying that for that damn thing. I could have picked it up on the side of the road.

Went back to that restaurant the next year. The owner said, "What will you give me for it?" I said, "Five hundred dollars." He said, "Sold." So we tied it onto that Jeep and had it covered up. We pull into a gas station with our kill that had been dead for twenty years and people gather around and ask, "Where you kill that at?"

"We shot it last night." We stood there talking and the gas kept pumping and overflowed that tank. It was running all over and the meter kept running. Can't put it back so we had to pay for it and got the hell out of there.

Everybody told me not to leave the phone company. They all said, "You are crazy to leave such a good job."

Dean is the best cook in the world. She can do green beans and potatoes, and they are terrific. Anything she puts her hands on, she makes it great.

Harrel and Joan are Lutheran. ELCA. They used to be Missouri Synod, but they switched. Harrel joined the Masons and the Missouri Synod does not approve of any kind of secret societies.

The Wheel & I guy invented the motor home, drove race cars, was a chef on TV, became wealthy and lived out all his fantasies. I never met him but I met a lot of his employees. This guy is like my guy Michaels, but Michaels, of course, never had the money to write a book, but just fun people.

Working with my brother was how we rose to the top. If he wanted to do something, we'd do it. If I wanted to something, same thing. It was like climbing a ladder back and forth. There was always something to keep me and him motivated. It was not quite the same with my other brothers. There must be something about being a twin that made us different. There is something that made us like that, how we could do everything together.

We both worked at Indiana Bell. When I told my sister we were quitting, she said, "You are going to starve to death."

(Harrel looked at an old picture.) Hey, look at that. That's Al Capone. That's my older brother. Doesn't he look like Al Capone?

Here's another picture. See that trailer there? I sold that trailer to some friends and they are still friends today. That was back in the '50s. They were the nicest people in the world. We still go to their farm to get eggs and cookies and noodles. She makes everything, all this good stuff. She is in her eighties now, eighty-two I think. Hardest-working woman you ever met. She'll still make them noodles today. She makes cookies, German cookies.

(Looking through more old photos.) Here's the first "sales lot" and little house, which is now a church. The writing on the windows is Harrel's advertising. Good old white shoe

polish. And sometimes he made his own concoction of flour and water.

Most people don't even know where to get off a wagon.

Look at Warren Buffet. He has all that money, but he is a simple man, a good-hearted guy. But he's a smart man. You know what his taxes were last year? Seventeen percent of his income. Seventeen percent of all those millions of dollars. Capital gains tax. The average guy going into the factory punching a time clock does not have any idea about capital gains or the tax rates. But rich people know how to do their taxes so they don't get killed. I have learned a lot, too. I buy city bonds. They put in sewer and water. And I get five percent interest on the money I invested. And I don't have to pay any federal tax on that interest. Tax-free municipal bonds have been a great thing for me. It helps the city and it helps me. The city gets the benefit of the cheaper loans.

I pay my share of taxes, don't get me wrong. But the guy punching a time clock, he gets paid and the taxes come out before he even sees his money. It's not fair to the working guy. It will never be fair.

(On politics.) I think Obama is going to do okay. My daughter, Karen, campaigned for Hillary Clinton, but we think Barack Obama will be all right. I got along okay with Bush. In fact, I voted for him. But I do not like his partner, Cheney. I don't like him. He does not have a heart in his body. He is the coldest guy I have ever seen interviewed in my life. He can't even look you in the face. He looks away from the camera; he can't even look anyone in the eye to talk to them. If a guy can't

look you in the eye and talk to you, you know, hell, he ain't any good. In my book, he ain't worth a shit. That is one of my pet peeves, you know. You go and talk to your husband and wife, and you can't look them in the eye, you know something ain't right.

The thing about this boy Obama is that he has a good heart and he will listen to people. I listen to other people. I could not do what I do or what I have done without other people. You have to be smart enough to know that you cannot do it all and you need help from other people to pick up in the areas that need doing.

I bought my first trailer up in Chicago. Stony Brook Avenue. Three thousand dollars. We hauled it back here and I sold it to a GI living out at Fort Harrison. We had more trouble with that damn trailer. It leaked, it was just awful. Then we bought another trailer, a better-quality one, to have on the lot. Joan and I lived in the little house, and Darrel and Shirley lived in the mobile home right there. We used it as a model home to show people. My brother's wife always kept it real nice and decorated real cute. We sold ten or twelve the first year. The next year we sold more than that.

One day he called me and asked if I would like to have five on display instead of one. I said, "I would love to but I don't have any money." He said, "I'll put them in there and when you sell them, you pay me for them." I said, "You're kidding me. Explain to me again what you just said." Nobody else would do something like that at all. I couldn't believe it. He told me he would put them on the lot and if it went over ninety days he would switch it out for another one. I figured I had nothing to lose doing that.

And that's what he said: "You've got nothing to lose. When you sell it, you have to pay me for it." Oh, I realize that. Obviously he believed in me to sell those mobile homes. He was right. One year, I sold fifty homes. My competitors would ask me, "What are you doing with all those damn expensive trailers on your lot?"

They were good homes. They would last and people loved them. They were like the Cadillac of mobile homes. They sold well and the customers would come back and thank me and everything else. So that's the guy who really put me on my feet.

Actually, I started out in the used trailer business. Buying and selling used mobile homes is the real beginning of the business. That was still in the days of working at the phone company. We would clean them up and paint them and fix whatever needed to be fixed. Darrel worked forty hours at the phone company and then another forty hours on this new mobile-home business.

Those days, they really were mobile homes and that name has stuck. "Manufactured homes" is a little too much for the mouth, or we are just creatures of habit, but back in those days, people would buy the mobile home from us and go to a sort of tourist camp. There was the hookup for the water dump and sewer, and they would park there. Oh, they would pay ten bucks or maybe twenty bucks a month to park there. They had to pump the water by hand and carry it back to their home.

Maybe they would stay a year and then haul it to another location. Now we have the mobile-home parks and people buy and live right here.

I knew how to work with people. It has always just been my instincts. If someone toured a home and liked it, but didn't like the carpet or the color of a room, I would simply ask if they would pay a little more to get what they did like. Oh, yeah, most of them would. The manufacturers were on a production line and did not make customer changes, but I could. And I did to make the sale.

I built the sales and my brother built the parks.

I had bank notes way back when at eighteen percent. I never thought interest rates would ever fall back below ten percent.

Computers have changed the world so much. I could run my business without a computer. But I know the banks, the airports, and hospitals all need to use the computer networks. They couldn't function without them.

You ever had a Bud Select? I drink one a day.

We built our house in 1973 for $28,000 and got seven acres of ground with it. We actually bought the land first and then about two years later built the house.

We never wanted for anything. I went to work at eight in the morning and would get home at nine or ten at night. I would run home to eat. I could go home at five to eat supper and be back to work in thirty minutes and stay until nine o'clock. Just about always came home for supper.

You always got to have your business card and a goddamn piece of paper.

I was a mean ol' son of a bitch when I was seventeen. I started driving a car when I was eleven years old. It was out in the country in Kentucky. We had gravel roads. I was born eighteen miles out of Bowling Green, which is a beautiful city, but we were out in the country. We raised tobacco. We had corn and beans. We grew everything that we ate. Strawberries. You name it—everything. We had cows we got our milk from. We had hogs that we got our pork from. We never went hungry. We always had plenty to eat. Poor as hell, though. And then my dad died when I was two. And my mother died when I was ten. It was rough, yes it was, but I just thank the Lord for being good to us. Everybody has been good to us.

Being twins, we drew attention. It is different from just being brothers. People are always comparing you when you're twins. See, I got a big mole behind my ear. And I remember people coming up to me and grabbing me and looking to see if I was the one who had the mole and then they would know my name.

Even now, as adults, we go to mobile-home shows and everyone knows us. Everyone knows the twins.

To be honest with you, I don't think my mom knew she was having twins. The doctor came to deliver a baby and I don't think either one of them knew there was two babies that she was carrying. That's just my personal belief; I really don't know, of course. I do know that she was a wonderful woman. Our mom was real good to us.

I like simple food. Always have. I still like my beans and corn bread. Country food. I don't eat so much red meat anymore, though, of course.

━━━

A conversation between Karen and Harrel:

Harrel: My daughter, Karen, has no stomach. She had to have surgery to have her stomach removed. She has no stomach. That operation scared the hell out of me. She had polyps. They had to take her whole stomach.

Karen: I had a husband and two daughters to live for, so I told the doctors to do whatever they had to do and when they woke me up after surgery, I would find out if I had part of a stomach or no stomach. Turns out the doctor decided he had to take it all. I have no stomach but you'd be amazed at how I can eat. If I were to meet you tomorrow at Le Peeps for breakfast you would see me eat like a normal person and never know that I did not have a stomach. In the beginning, right after surgery, I had to eat small portions and not big meals. Small amounts of food all during the day. I always make sure I eat my protein. I can't eat a lot of sugar.

Harrel: We did a lot of praying through that deal.

Karen: We had a lot going on all about the same time. I had my surgery and Dad found out about his liver thing, and then Mom was diagnosed with breast cancer. We thought, wow, how can all three of us being going through something at the same time?

Harrel: It has been five or six years for me. I think I was diagnosed with cancer about six years ago. I had it in the kidney. I had to have a kidney taken out, and then it spread. But all in all, I have been in good health until this past year.

Karen: We've been through some real ups and downs, I guess. It helps to have a strong faith in God. And we have a pretty close family. We all have pretty good relationships.

Harrel: Yeah, and one boss.

Karen: Yeah, he's our main boss. We laugh a lot. We're a pretty tight-knit family.

———

Darrel and I were in first grade, at that little, one-room school. I don't remember much of that time, but I do remember that we had plays. We had a Christmas play and I couldn't remember my part. Darrel could remember his lines, but I couldn't remember mine. Leon—I think it was Leon, anyway—took my place in that Christmas play. Did you know that I flunked second grade. They held me back. Not that it really mattered, because we were all in that classroom together, just independently working on our classwork for our own grade level and at our own pace.

In the third grade, I remember, that was when my mom died. I remember Darrel and I being in class and they sent for us at school. We walked across the field. We walked along the path we had made as a shortcut. We were there with her when she passed away. She died shortly after we got home. She had been sick and had lung trouble and the doctor had given her a shot that was just too much for her heart to handle.

I think it was third grade when Darrel fell off a log and broke his arm. Darrel says that I decided to wear a sling on my arm, too, but I don't really remember that. But I do know that Darrel did break his arm at school.

From third grade to, I suppose, about the eighth grade, I had the same teacher, Mrs. Mary Maxy. She just lived down the foot of the hill from the school. She took a liking to Darrel and me. Mrs. Maxy had a daughter who went to school with us, too. She was a real good-looking girl. She ended up marrying a good friend of mine.

Those were good times, even though I can't say I ever really liked school. I liked my friends and I liked Mrs. Maxy. Then, after eighth grade, Darrel and I came up here to Indianapolis.

Third grade through that time into eighth grade, we lived with our brother, Paul. Dean had moved up here to Indy.

Walter then had to go into the service, so Dean came down and lived with us. Walter, he was a real nice guy. Anyway, it worked out that Paul married Mary and they needed newly-wed privacy, and Walter and Dean were in Indy so we went up to live with them. The first thing off the bat, we went out looking for stuff to do. We were never lazy.

I walked up to the grocery store on the corner. They had a little trailer park there. There was a gas station there, too. I will never forget that day I walked up to old Mike Michaels and told him I wanted a job, that I wanted to work there for him. That day really did change my life.

We would have the wholesalers come in to sell us their groceries. They were always bullshitters. A lot of fun, but bullshitters. Mike's wife was a great worker. She took care of all the paperwork. Mike was not a good detail person. He never picked up a pencil. I don't think I ever saw him with one in all my life. Mike was a good man and a good worker, too, except for his one problem: whiskey. He got hooked on it. But he was a great guy and had a great heart. I only knew this wife, who was actually his second wife. His fist wife had died sometime before I ever met him. He had a son by the first wife and two little girls the second.

I remember at that time you could get by on $350 a month. You could make a house payment, a car payment and buy your gasoline. You didn't need any more income. You could get by on that if you were conservative.

Now, of course, everything is different. And now with this economy. Boy, I don't know what to say. I do know to tell people to enjoy their money. Spend it. Do what makes you happy. Go hunting. Go fishing. I miss my fishing. Just being out there is good. It frees up your mind whether you catch any fish at all.

Michaels got sick with asthma and had to move to Phoenix, to dry weather. His partner was a guy named Greenwall.

I never liked school. I don't think I tried to really learn a lot because I always knew that I had to go to work. I wasn't a good reader. That makes school a lot more difficult. Every class is harder when you don't like to read. But I guess I did like high school. I liked high school better than grammar school. I tried out for football when I came up here for high school. I was big. But you know, I kept thinking I could be working and making fifty cents an hour. I could work ten hours and make five bucks.

That's what took my interest away from any sports. And really, I was never that big of a sports fan. I didn't hate sports, but it was not my passion. I didn't have to have tickets to games or anything like that. It was not as big as it is now. Sporting events are a big deal now.

The thing about coming to school up here, although it was so different and so much bigger than what we were used to, that one-room school building to having maybe 100 kids in our graduating class, was that it didn't take long to make friends if you were nice. I had some good friends in high school. We had a lot of fun and didn't get into trouble. Not any serious trouble, anyway. You know, there may have been a car wreck or some mischievous stuff that I shouldn't have done. But it was more or less accident kind of stuff. I knew that if I got into serious trouble that I didn't have anyone to get me out of it.

I had to work and to earn my way, I knew that. Dean and Walter were always good to me and provided me food and a place to live. But as far as a lot of luxuries, we didn't have those. But we had all the same as most people did back then. Had an automobile. Darrel and I always had an automobile. We got our first pickup truck in 1948 or 1949. We pulled trailers and hauled junk. We would charge people to clean their yards up. About anything you could make any money with, we were willing to do it.

One summer, this guy we knew got us both jobs at a place called Bridgeport Brass. They paid around a dollar and a half per hour. Pretty damn good pay back then. We worked there all summer. Darrel's boss got killed there one night. Something fell and stabbed him right in the lung. Darrel said, "To hell with this." That was the end of that.

We were down in Kentucky at some kind of homecoming or picnic. This guy down there had his brother in from Louisville. He was driving a brand-new Ford convertible. Yeah, it was Charles Guffy's brother. There was a gravel pit up there about seven or eight miles. We went swimming in it. After we left the gravel pit we were all going off to someplace else, I can't even remember, and they all said, "Harrel you're the best driver." They told me to drive. Four or five of us jumped into that convertible and drove off down that gravel road.

We were going too fast. We hit some gravel. We hit gravel in the middle of the road and that son of a bitch went sideways.

We lost control and went into the woods and hit a goddamn tree. It was as big as that tree there. We of course had the top down. Damn, the blood was flying out this kid's head. His head hit something and blood was all over the place. I was scared to death. He ended up okay, but it did a number on me. I was shook up and did not sleep at all that night. It stayed with me for a long time.

That boy who cut his head was Frank Miller. We were all maybe sixteen. I was scared to go back to visit Kentucky after that. I don't know if I had my driver's license then or not. It didn't matter back then.

They had to get a tractor to get the car pulled out of the woods. That brand-new car. I guess his brother ended up getting the car fixed. It didn't cost me a nickel, that's all I know. It sure taught me to slow down. I know people tell you that, and I tell my kids and grandkids that. Sometimes a kid has to go through it himself. Those f***ing trees are not made out of rubber.

(When asked about the Army, Harrel says he got out of high school and since Dean was working at General Motors, she was able to get him a job.) It would have been a good job, but then the draft came along. They drafted our asses off to the Army. I didn't like the Army. They screamed at me like I was nothing. I was a codgy SOB and I didn't like anybody screaming at me. I knew I was not going to stay in the Army.

Some of the guys were bullshitters like me, and some guys sat around reading their Bibles. I did everything from company carpenter to working on oil furnaces. We got put on a ship off to Korea and on the way, they announced the war was over and we were going to Japan. Darrel became a cook. I didn't know shit about working on oil furnaces, but I told them that I did.

Darrel sold his pass to some kid for five dollars. That kid didn't show up for reveille the next morning. So they tracked Darrel down because this kid had gotten in trouble and it was Darrel's information on the pass. The powers in charge put Darrel on KP duty. Washing dishes and that kind of stuff. There was a guy in the kitchen who was kind of like Michaels. He got Darrel a job as a cook. He and Darrel got along real well. Darrel became a good cook.

We both like to cook. In the end, the Army wanted us both to reenlist and be cooks. I pretty much said, "F*** you, I am not staying in this Army." So we got out of the Army and went back to Indy and went to work for Michaels. I did not like the Army at all because somebody was always telling you what to do. I didn't like to take orders. I was a mean little fu****. I didn't like to take orders from anybody then and really, I still don't like to today. I was a cocky little cocker, I hate to admit it.

(Harrel likes telling the story of his short-lived antiques business.) I had bought a lot of mobile homes through Morris Plan and the guy I worked with, who did all that financing with me, he was quite a big wheel. He was over my head but I was doing well and making money and one day I was in his office and he asked me if I wanted to make good bucks. I said, "Hell yes." He said he had a whole schoolhouse full of antiques. He wanted to open an antiques store. He said, "We'll go in halves and

we'll split it." He said, "You give me some money and I'll put it together." I asked, "How much money you talking about?" He said $7,000, but my share was just half of that.

I said okay and decided to go down and see these antiques. I didn't want to mention it to Darrel because we had always been in business together. But I figured, hell, it ain't his call. So I didn't want to get a check made out still, so I went over the bank and drew out cash—$3750. Joan and I had four thousand in the bank at that time. I gave him that cash. In pencil on his business card was the only note or contract we drew up.

Time goes by and I find out this guy, John, who is also in the mobile-home business is the other half owner of this antiques deal. I knew John was a real nice guy. I knew him from mobile-home shows. Darrel and I were going to buy out his business, actually. We were going to make a deal with him. We would be seventy-five percent and he would be twenty-five percent. And I remember one day asking Darrel, "What is seventy-five percent of nothing?" And he said, "Nothing." That is what we got out of that deal.

We had ventures on the side from time to time and some went well and some did not go so well. And as for that antiques business, I never saw a dime. I never got paid back for my investment and I didn't make any money from that deal.

Darrel found that piece of ground out on Post Road next to Fort Harrison. We thought we could get it and make it in into a nice mobile-home park. We needed to make $300,000 to get it, and that was a lot of money back then. Darrel knows more about it than I do. We bought a farm and traded that farm to get that land. Then, of course, we had to get it zoned. Damn trouble with that sometimes.

Well, I went to Speedway Bank to get a loan. They tell me that I need to get a CPA and an attorney. I said, "Hell, what do I need either one of them for?" The guy at the bank said that they would put together a financial statement and a certified audit. I asked what that was all about. The banker said the CPA would verify all my assets and if they lie, they are the ones in trouble. Basically, I needed the CPA and attorney to tell the banker that I really had that much money and that I was good for a loan. My word was not good enough.

So I asked the banker, "Where do I find one of these fu****s?" He gave me the name of Bob Lichtenhauer. Bob was a real nice guy, an easygoing cowboy. Not real aggressive in finances, but just a hell of an honest guy. He hooked us up with Bob Whipple. He walked in and he was a real professional. He was bald-headed little guy. He was well known in town as a good CPA. I didn't know if he had a wife or kids but he was good CPA and put together my financial statements for me. He did it all perfect, you know.

So I took my financial statements and the attorney letters and everything the bank had asked for. I went back down to the bank. I had to end up getting some damn life insurance, too, but we did end up getting the bank loan. And we got that mobile-home park and were able to pay back that whole loan in five or six years.

In the beginning, we made our profit on the mobile-home sales. Now it is reversed. It used to be the sales funded the parks, and now it is the parks—the lot rent—that gives the business the profit. From a business point of view, I want people to understand that. Business is always changing and we knew we had to keep up with the changes. And now our boys are doing the same. Adapting to the needs of now. Real smart boys we've got running the show now.

Bob was a great attorney and a great guy. Bob Whipple was a great CPA for us. He was a great golfer around town. I never cared for golf, but I know a lot of people do.

We came from a very, very small town. We have come a long way in a lot of different ways, really, but we always still felt and acted like the way we were brought up. People call it Southern hospitality. We just know it as treating people right, and having a little fun along the way.

Epilogue

The writer who helped us compile these stories and put it all into book form was impressed with our dads and how they relate to everyone that they come into contact with. After her initial visit, she wrote a column that appeared in many small newspapers all across the country. Because of the confidentiality agreement that was signed, a standard contract for ghostwriters, she did not name names. We would like to print that column here as a closing tribute to our fathers, Harrel Cohron and Darrel Cohron.

—Brad Cohron, Bobby Cohron

I'm in Indianapolis meeting with clients and gathering information for the book they want written. As a ghostwriter, I can't divulge much about the people I meet or the books I write, but these guys probably won't mind if I refer to them in the abstract.

This is a classic "rags to riches" story. Every such story is as individual and unique to the parties it belongs to, and this one belongs to two individuals—twins. These two gentlemen are now 76. After years of having folks tell them, "You should write a book," they decided what the heck, why not.

Hal and Dale (not their real names; I changed the names to protect the innocent, namely me, so I don't get into trouble with my confidentiality contract) are a true American success story. They were born in on a farm in Kentucky. Their father died when they were two, and their mother died when they were ten.

They were raised by older siblings, moved to Indy with their eldest sister and her husband, and were later drafted to serve in the Korean War. The day they shipped out was the day the war ended. Timing has continued to be on their side.

The two went into business together in 1955 and have created a multimillion dollar empire. Their company still thrives today under the leadership and management of their sons. A grandson from the third generation has now entered the business as well.

In 1955, family owned businesses were the norm. Today, they're a rarity. Even more amazing is that there is no rivalry, feuding, or power struggles among the second generation who has taken over the helm. There's tales of rock throwing and fist fights between the twins (as adults at company "board meetings"), but they always respected each other and relied on each other.

I made the comment that being in business with family is hard. Hal agreed and stated, "If it was just my brother, I couldn't do it, but he's my twin. It's different."

Something else that strikes me as being different really should not, but in our corporate world today of greed and corruption, it is sad that decency actually seems different. Hal and Dale started their business practicing the golden rule and they have it in their company brochures to this day.

Loyalty and trust are the backbones to success. Financial success takes hard work, certainly, and they put in long hours for a lot of years, but they have always operated under that one main premise: Do unto others as you would have them do unto you.

"It's just common sense," this family tells me. Sure, but common sense and common courtesy sometimes seem to be hallmarks of a bygone era. I'm not the only who thinks so. I'm also writing a book for a powerhouse Canadian business leader who believes that the missing ingredient in today's business management is the fact that people matter.

Hal and Dale have never lost sight of that fact. The company motto is We Love People. "I stole that motto from a rental car company years ago," Hal says. Maybe so, but I've never felt loved when I was stuck waiting in line at a rental car place.

People feel loved here. Their customers, suppliers, and employees are faithful; their loyalty is earned and returned. One word that keeps popping up in interviews is compassion. Empathy also seems like a lost attribute sometimes. It's alive and well here in this family business in Indy.

Every life, every person has a story to tell; I'm glad I get to tell theirs.